DATE DUE			

Law of the Sea

AN SMU LAW SCHOOL STUDY

LAW OF
THE SEA

Oceanic Resources

ERIN BAIN JONES

Preface by
SCOTT CARPENTER

Foreword by
CHARLES O. GALVIN

SOUTHERN METHODIST UNIVERSITY PRESS • DALLAS

© 1972 • Southern Methodist University Press • Dallas

Library of Congress Catalog Card Number: 72-96510

ISBN Number: 0-87074-134-9

CONTENTS

FOREWORD

DURING the 1960s we achieved the national goal of placing a man on the moon and thus opened a new frontier for all mankind—the exploration and utilization of the limitless resources of outer space. In this same period we became conscious of the extent to which we as a people are despoiling our land. New studies in ecology and environment have led to state and national legislation for the better protection of our resources of water, air, and natural beauty. The ominous threat of diminishing supplies of fuel and energy has impelled us to experiment with new techniques of providing power and of conserving known supplies. It has also encouraged the exploration of vast areas of our world not previously considered as practically available. Oil and gas exploration began in the North Sea, the Canadian Arctic, and elsewhere as man perfected techniques for tapping energy reserves not heretofore accessible.

And so our attention has turned to the seas—those vast areas over which men have traversed the earth's surface since before recorded history but whose mineral and nutritional riches have eluded our successful utilization except to a relatively limited extent. The possibility of vast stores of valuable minerals and food supplies sets the stage for the consideration of extraordinarily difficult problems of rights, ownership, access, and the other legal paraphernalia with which competing sovereign states must deal.

Dr. Jones has made a significant contribution to the state of the knowledge, for she has carefully examined the history of the developing law in this area and the evolving critical questions of property rights in the seabed and its subsoil. She has provided an excellent conceptual analysis of current efforts at satisfactory resolution of the problems through international organizations and multilateral international arrangements. Her knowledge of the technical problems as they apply to the difficult legal matters makes her a respected authority in the field. She has participated extensively in scientific conferences, and she was selected to accompany recent scientific expeditions to the Arctic and Antarctic.

It is a privilege for me to write this foreword to pay tribute to a distinguished lawyer and scholar for her unceasing and unstinting efforts in breaking through to new frontiers of the law. More especially, however, I am honored to count her as a friend and colleague, a gracious gentlewoman who has an unselfish devotion to quality in scholarship and education.

CHARLES O. GALVIN

School of Law
Southern Methodist University
November, 1972

PREFACE

A QUARTER OF A CENTURY AGO, the vast expanses of the world's oceans were considered important mainly for defense, fishing, and navigation. Today it is recognized that they are one of the last unexploited areas of this planet, and capable of far-reaching contributions to the well-being of all mankind. Our twentieth-century technological development has given us the capacity to employ the oceans and their resources for an ever increasing variety of uses with an ever increasing intensity. Concomitant with this advance in the use of the oceans has come the increasing capability of destroying their usefulness by over-fishing, pollution, or wasteful use of their mineral resources.

The present status of the law of the sea, therefore, is of vital importance not only to the international lawyer or those interested in national defense or foreign affairs, but also to scientists, ecologists, explorers of the deep, and business entrepreneurs.

Dr. Erin Bain Jones bears these multiple audiences in mind as she traces the history of the law of the seas from its earliest origins up to the crises of today which revolve about the legal problems facing those who seek to utilize our new capabilities to extract from the oceans the hidden riches of petroluem, minerals, and foodstuffs so vital to a world of exploding populations and industrially developing societies.

It would be impossible for me to write this brief foreword without touching upon Dr. Jones's unique personal qualities. She possesses the rare quality of being vitally interested in people from all professions and from all walks of life. Her intellectual horizons are boundless, extending from vast outer space to deep inner space. Her mature consideration of her fellow man, her balanced judgment, her integrity and charm, have earned her the respect and affection of all who have come in contact with her.

Scott Carpenter

Los Angeles, California
November 8, 1972

ACKNOWLEDGMENTS

FOR THE PRIVILEGE of exploring the subject of this book, I wish to thank Dean Charles O. Galvin, School of Law, Southern Methodist University.

I gratefully acknowledge my indebtedness to Professor A. J. Thomas, Jr., and Professor Ann Van Wynen Thomas for prolonged assistance in serving as advisers for the manuscript.

Also, for almost daily assistance during a period of five years, I thank librarians at Southern Methodist University School of Law, Miss Hibernia Turbeville, Mrs. Carolyn Hoffman, Baroness Nada Smit, Miss Sue Albright, Mrs. Billie Brooks.

Other acknowledgments include assistance and courtesies from individuals, librarians, and institutions: Dr. Richard A. Geyer, Director of Oceanography, Texas A. & M. University; Professor Roy R. Ray, Southern Methodist University School of Law; Gifford Johnson, Southwest Center for Advanced Studies of The University of Texas System; Sir Edward C. Bullard, Cambridge University; Dr. Thomas F. Gaskell, Scientific Adviser, British Petroleum Company, London; Eric Arthur, British Petroleum Company, London; and Lieutenant Commander

Scott Carpenter, Deep Submergence Systems Project, Chevy Chase, Maryland, Department of the Navy. I am appreciative of assistance at the following libraries: Bodleian Law Library and Radcliffe Science Library (Department of the Bodleian Library, Oxford, England); Library of the British Museum; The Law Library of The University of London; The United Nations Economic and Social Council (UNES-CO), Paris; Bibliothèque Nationale, Paris; Musée Oceanographique de Monaco.

ERIN BAIN JONES

Dallas, Texas
November, 1972

Law of the Sea

CHAPTER ONE

INTRODUCTION

THE WORLD OCEAN captivated the interest of intrepid navigators of previous centuries. Phoenicians, Vikings, Christopher Columbus and others ventured upon the sea in quest of undiscovered lands. To these courageous adventurers, the oceans were a means of passage for voyages of unknown duration and dangers—to unknown shores. In the sixteenth century Ferdinand Magellan's hazardous voyage led to the circumnavigation of the globe, and in the eighteenth Captain James Cook's successful explorations of the Pacific Ocean resulted in the charting of the ocean's vast realm, covering approximately two-thirds of the surface of the planet Earth.[1] Subsequently, expeditions were initiated to gain knowledge of the sea itself.

New interest in oceanography was stimulated in 1866, when the transatlantic cable was laid.[2]

In contrast to the endeavors of previous years, oceanographers of the twentieth century are engaged in downward probes into the oceans, penetrating the sedimentary carpet covering the floor of the sea, and into rocks below the sediment.[3] The actual depths of the world ocean and the contour of the ocean floor were of negligible

interest until the mid-nineteenth century, when initial scientific surveys
were made. The most significant expedition of this period was that of
the British ship H.M.S. *Challenger* which resulted in over two hundred soundings,[4] including a record sounding of 4500 fathoms made
only 50 miles from the deepest part of the ocean, and in the discovery
of the existence of phosphorite and concretionary manganese dioxide
deposits on the ocean floor. For many years these discoveries were
of no more than scientific interest. Even the economic significance of
offshore mining of petroleum, which had its origin in 1899, was
relatively small. Undersea deposits of hard minerals, such as coal or
iron, were mined before the twentieth century by a tunnel system
from adjacent land. The seabed and its subsoil were of minor importance until the termination of World War II. During this period,
however, economic, political, and legal interests were limited to the
land beneath the shallow waters of the continental shelf; deeper
waters were considered to have only one practical usage, the support
of submarine pipes and cables. As late as 1956, the ocean floor lacked
justification for regulation.

In recent years, a multitude of endeavors have ushered in a
reversal in attitudes. There has been an increasing awareness of the
significance of the ocean and its resources to man's well-being and
even survival.[5] Accelerated technological progress has made feasible
the discovery of mineral resources on and beneath the ocean floor,
and has made these resources accessible and exploitable for diverse
purposes. Previously, a primitive, laborious method of dredging and
weighted lines was employed to acquire limited knowledge of the
seabed.

Today, phenomenally improved underwater photography and television, as well as the echo-sounder, reveal an accurate picture of the
shape of the sea floor with its impressive topography of mountainous
areas approximating the height of the Himalayas, canyons comparable
to the Grand Canyon, expansive plains and valleys. A great variety of
sophisticated devices has been developed; seismic tests have been
successfully made. The scanning sonar provides a precise and accurate
image of the ocean floor. These devices also disclose indications of
the irregularities of geological structures on the submerged land.
Ninety per cent of the ocean floor remains unknown; knowledge of
this area beyond the geophysical continental shelf is meager and

fragmentary.[6] Within a period of fifteen years, however, knowledge has been greatly increased. There are reliable indications of virtually inexhaustible mineral resources within the oceanic reservoir; it is, therefore, predicted that it will be one of the major sources of supply for the world's mineral requirements. At the surface of the Pacific Ocean floor alone the quantity of manganese nodules is ample to yield sufficient manganese, copper, nickel, cobalt and other indispensable minerals to provide abundantly for the anticipated world demand for thousands of years at the present rate of consumption. In some instances, also, the present rate of mineral accumulation in the seas exceeds the present rate of consumption.

THE NATURE OF THE PROBLEM

The sea's mineral resources pose major problems for future solutions. The initial problem concerns the devising of methods of collecting in quantity the rich mineral deposits from the sea floor. The second problem is to discover the processes by which plants and animals consolidate minerals from sea water. When these complex processes have found solutions, man-made concentrating equipment may be devised to extract at least a portion of the existing minerals. The sea is regarded as the last great natural frontier remaining on the planet Earth. It has an immeasurable, incalculable reservoir of wealth in the form of power which engineers ambitiously propose to utilize for the construction of huge dams to influence enormous weather changes and attain other advantageous objectives. Soviet engineers, for example, calculate that a Bering Straits dam, equipped with batteries of large pumps, could substantially alter the severity of climatic conditions.

Another problem is related to a proper assessment of the total deposits located in the sea, to distribution of the deposits in various geological localities, and to scientific inquiries concerning the complexity of oceanic phenomena, together with the approximate rate of accumulation for industrially significant elements in these deposits. Still another problem has to do with efforts to categorize the various mineral environmental factors of the sea's continental shelves, seawater, marine beaches, and subsea hard rock. Thus, power, food, and mineral deposits beyond computation await the exploitation of the nations of the Earth when sufficient knowledge of the seas' potentiality is revealed by adequate technological methods of recovery. And of importance to all humanity will be the legal regime which must eventually evolve to govern the exploitation of the wealth of the seas.

As an aid to the understanding of the present world position in the development of such a regime, let us review the historical legal concepts of various nations concerning freedom of the seas.

Past Views of Law for Oceanic Areas
ROMAN

Roman law propounded the dictum that the sea as well as the shores of the sea were common to all, and that the right of fishing in rivers and ports was in like manner free to all; that animals, *ferae naturae*, including fish, belonged to no one.[7] Hugo Grotius, in his consideration of the freedom of water, cited Roman authors, among them Cicero, who admonished that no one should be deprived of the water that flows by. Ovid declared that the world of water was free to all, that Nature made neither sun nor air nor water private property but rather made them public gifts, belonging to human society as a whole. Grotius continued that the air belongs in this same category, as it is insusceptible of occupation; moreover, its common use is destined for all men. For similar reasons, the sea is common to all, because its limitless expanses cannot become a possession of anyone, and because it is adapted for the utilization of all, whether for navigational purposes or for fishing privileges. Virgil also stated that the air, the sea, and the shore are open for all men.[8]

MIDDLE AGES

Prior to the end of the thirteenth century, Venice, eminent in commercial activities, affluence, and maritime power, assumed sovereignty over the entire Adriatic, though possession of both shores was lacking. Tributes were levied on ships which navigated the gulf, or passage of ships was prohibited. Adjacent cities and commonwealths were compelled to agree to the demands of Venice, which were ultimately recognized by other European powers and by the Pope.[9] The Republic of Genoa enforced a similar claim to dominion of the Ligurian Sea. Other Mediterranean states followed the confiscatory policy of appropriation regarding waters with which they were concerned. The assumption of sovereign jurisdiction was advantageous to navigation and commerce, in that perilous era of anarchy which prevailed after the dissolution of the Roman empire. Depredation and lawlessness were constant hazards. In the thirteenth century the duty of exercising supremacy of admiralty jurisdiction on the adjacent sea became a prerogative of sovereign power. It was a natural assumption of sovereignty of the sea on the part of the great cities of Italy which controlled important east-west shipping. Italian jurists attempted to give legal sanction to the practice.

In like manner, in the north of Europe, Denmark, Sweden, and subsequently Poland contested for or participated in the dominion of the Baltic. Scandinavian claims to maritime supremacy are probably among the most significant in history.[10]

Turbulence accompanied the era, wars ensued. Claims resulted in many international treaties concerning disputes related to trading, navigation and fisheries.

JURIDICAL CONTROVERSIES CONCERNING MARE LIBERUM AND MARE CLAUSUM

The comprehensive claims set forth by Spain and Portugal in the sixteenth century produced far-reaching consequences. These two powers divided the great oceans between them by authority granted to them by papal edict. Spain's claim included the exclusive right of navigation in the western Atlantic, in the Gulf of Mexico, and in the Pacific. Similarly, Portugal claimed the Atlantic south of Morocco and the Indian Ocean. These exaggerated pretensions to dominion over the great waters of the globe resulted in prolonged juridical controversies over the doctrines of *Mare Liberum*[11] and *Mare Clausum*.[12]

Sixteenth-century authors who considered the question of appropriation of the seas accepted the dictum that the seas were capable of appropriation and that they were under the sovereignty of some power. Only infrequently were protests raised against the exclusive maritime dominion of Venice, Portugal, or Spain.

In 1609 a slender book, *Mare Liberum*, appeared anonymously, the unknown author's objective being to oppose the pretensions of Portuguese navigational and commercial monopolistic practices in this region. His argument restricted the application of his *Mare Liberum* doctrine to the open sea. His major premise was to establish the right of the Dutch to trade with the Indies.

PAPAL

A number of fifteenth-century Papal Bulls were significant in influencing concepts regarding freedom of the sea.

In 1493 Pope Alexander VI (Rodrigo Borgia) issued a Bull purporting to apportion the undiscovered areas of the world between Spain and Portugal by an imaginary line drawn from the North Pole to the South Pole west of the Azores and Cape Verde Islands for one hundred leagues. (The following year the line was diverted to the west by the Treaty of Tordesillas made by the sovereigns of the two countries.)[13] The Papal Bulls had far-reaching repercussions in that they not only made no attempt at limitation of the right of the two sovereigns to grant title to the newly acquired territories, but also encompassed the prohibition of all commerce at sea except by license issued by Spanish or Portuguese authorities.[14] The drastic effect of the Bulls was that the two powers claimed flagrant privileges of monopoly of navigational and commercial enterprises with both the New World and the East Indies[15] These claims constituted a formidable barrier to trade with other nations. The Papal Bulls as well as the rights of discovery, occupation, and conquest, formed the foundations for the titles of these vast regions. Thus, through the grant by Pope Alexander VI, Spain and Portugal arrogated to their domain the exclusive sovereignty of the great oceans which provided passage to these illimitable regions—the Atlantic, the Indian Ocean, and areas of the Pacific.[16] These two countries vigorously enforced the exclusive rights conferred upon them by the Pope. Harsh measures, the death penalty or confiscation of goods, were imposed for navigation to their new possessions or for trading, or dealing in commerce, without royal license. Thus, through Papal grant two nations controlled these areas to the exclusion of all other nations.

Pope Alexander VI exercised his temporal power once again in 1493, when, upon the return of Christopher Columbus from his first voyage, by a Bull to the Spanish monarchs he gave confirmation to their rights in the new territory. Various Papal Bulls were also granted to Queen Elizabeth I to secure her possessions,[17] but these were far less significant than previous Papal edicts.

DUTCH

In the early seventeenth century the ambitious Dutch endeavored to divert a portion of the Indies' wealth to northern Europe, despite the issuance of the Papal Bull of 1493 which reserved this area as Portuguese domain. Controversies resulted; the eminent Dutch scholar and jurist, Hugo Grotius,[18] was solicited as a young advocate by the Dutch East India Company to prepare a defense of the trading policy with the East. He wrote his defense, *De Jure Praedae*, in 1605. In November, 1609, he published as a separate pamphlet one chapter of this work (the twelfth), *Mare Liberum*, a tractate in defense of the right of the Dutch or any other nation to participate actively in the East Indian trade.

In establishing his thesis of the freedom of the seas, Grotius cited ancient writers with approbation, stating that the high seas were not within the sovereignty of any state, and therefore navigation in the high seas was open to the ships of all nations.[19]

The arguments presented by the Portuguese to lend justification to their claim were attacked by Grotius. He maintained the invalidity of their claim for titles from prior discovery of the Cape route, under Papal Bulls, and by right of conquest or war, as well as from prescriptive claim or from occupancy.[20] Grotius encouraged the Dutch to assert their rights by an exercise of force. He made a larger appeal "to the civilized world for complete freedom of the high seas for the innocent use and mutual benefit of all."[21] He relied upon statements in conformity with Roman law, on the law of nature and of nations, and included elevated moral values. He sought to defend the origin of the acquisition of property from primitive times when all things were held in common ownership; he differentiated between private and public property and what is common. All property, he asserted, is based upon possession or occupation, which requires that all movables shall be seized and all immovables shall be enclosed; things which cannot be seized nor be subject to enclosure may not become property: they are common to all, and their usage pertains to the entire human race rather than to a particular people.[22] Air is common because it cannot be occupied and is not exhaustible by use; it is designated, therefore, as belonging to all mankind. Similarly, the sea is common to all. It is infinite, in a sense, is incapable of being possessed, and is appropriate for the use of all for navigational and commerical purposes and for fishing privileges. It belongs to all and may not be subject to appropriation by any one.

The opinions which were reiterated by Grotius in *Mare Liberum* as to the free use of the sea were included in his greatest work, *The Rights of War and Peace*, published in 1625.[23]

Mare Liberum was published to achieve recognition of the right of the Dutch to sail to the East Indies and to engage in trade and commercial enterprises there. This right was accomplished by the treaty of Antwerp within the month after its appearance in March, 1609.[24]

Juridical controversies concerning the appropriation and dominion of the seas existed throughout the seventeenth century and continued into the eighteenth.[25] By the Grotian view of the law of nations, however, navigation is free to all persons. "Every nation is free to travel to every other nation and to engage in trade with it."[26]

BRITISH

Concurrently with other nations, Britain directed its attention to customs relative to the sea, after voyages of discovery necessitated reexamination of the dichotomous question. Inquiries were posed as to national jurisdiction of the high seas and whether the oceans were indeed subject to appropriation as the exclusive property of a particular state or states.

In 1580 Queen Elizabeth asserted the freedom of the seas as a definitive principle of the Law of Nations, in her edict that the sea and the air were open and free to all mankind, and that no exclusive rights in them could be obtained by given nations or individuals.[27]

When the sovereignty of the British seas became a topic of international significance in the seventeenth century, the English crown employed eminent scholars and jurists to search for evidence to support its antiquity.

During this century, English pretensions to the sovereignty of the sea were supported by the erudite scholar John Selden, who attempted to establish that the sovereigns of England from remote antiquity had exercised exclusive dominion and jurisdiction over the surrounding seas of England as part of its territory. He endeavored to establish that the sea is capable of appropriation and that in numerous instances it had been appropriated. Logical objections to his doctrine were interposed: first, that it is opposed to the law of nature and the law of nations to forbid free commerce and navigation; second, that the physical nature of the sea prohibits its occupation. Learned authorities objected to his theoretical doctrines. He sought to prove that the practice and custom of both modern and ancient nations established that the sea was indeed capable of private dominion, and therefore such appropriation was not violative of the law of nature or nations. He cited modern nations to reenforce his thesis—among them the Venetians in the Adriatic, the Genoese in the Ligurian Sea, the Spaniards and Portuguese, as well as the maritime dominion of the Danes and Norwegians, the Poles and the Turks, possessing sovereignty in the Baltic and Black Seas respectively.[28]

Selden continued his argument for the British position to the effect that maritime sovereignty had been in continuous practice by the ancient Britons, the Romans, and the Anglo-Saxons in succession, and by the Normans and subsequent kings. He relied upon a multitude of references from documents to establish his argument that the kings of England had perpetually exercised exclusive dominion and jurisdiction in the adjacent seas as a portion of their domain; he contended that they had preserved the privilege of prohibiting fishing and navigation by foreigners within the British seas, and had required tribute for the right; he further concluded that the rights of the Crown in the surrounding seas had been claimed by kings and parliaments and were, therefore, in accord with the common law of England, and that in many respects these rights had received recognition by other nations.[29] Selden's assertions of the maritime sovereignty of the kings of England were relative and were absolute in character.[30]

In 1635 Selden dedicated his book, Mare Clausum, to the King. The book had been written sixteen or seventeen years prior to this date, but its publication had been forbidden by James I for political reasons. Mare Clausum, therefore, appeared approximately twenty-five years after Grotius's Mare Liberum. Selden's authoritative work was relied upon by leading advocates to establish both the existence and the legality of the right of the sovereigns of England to jurisdiction over the British seas. Selden's conception and definition of the extent of those seas predominated in recognized treatises on the law of England as late as 1830.[31] His scholarly exposition of the right of the crown of England in the British seas, although superior to other works which were written on the subject,[32] nevertheless did not settle the juridical controversies attached to appropriation and dominion of the surrounding seas; for debate continued with unabated persistence into the eighteenth and nineteenth centuries.[33]

TWENTIETH CENTURY

Retrospectively, the doctrine advocating freedom of the seas was enunciated in 1509 by the celebrated Spanish jurist de Vitoria and defended by Vasquez de Menchaca; yet it was Grotius who is credited with establishing the principle upon an unassailable legal foundation.[34] Ultimately his views prevailed over Selden's theories advanced in *Mare Clausum*. Lord Stowell, in the case of *Le Louis* (1817)[35] synthesized the rationale: "All nations have an equal right to the unappropriated parts of the ocean for their navigation." Judge Story, in the *Marianna Flora* case, commented—"Upon the ocean, in time of peace, all possess an entire equality. It is the common highway of all, appropriated to the use of all, and no one can vindicate to himself a superior or exclusive prerogative there."[36] Fauchille commented: "The high sea does not form part of the territory of any State. No State can have over it a right of ownership, sovereignty, or jurisdiction. None can lawfully claim to dictate laws for the high seas."[37] Thus there were indications that the epoch of claims to exclusive sovereignty over extensive regions of the sea had not only materially diminished but had been superseded by the definitive concept of the freedom of the open seas.

Twentieth-century doctrine, in like manner, accepts the legal dictum of the custom of the nations and principles of international law to the effect that the open ocean may not be appropriated by any one power and is free and open to all nations for all purposes. Nevertheless, it is established that all states possess soverign rights in the areas of the sea adjacent to their shores, although there is not, and has not been, general agreement as to the exact nature of those rights, or as to the dimension of the sea belt which may be so appropriated.[38] The exclusive rights of maritime states in the waters adjacent to their coasts are not only recognized but clearly embodied in international law.[39]

The area of the sea along the coasts of respective nations which could be protected or controlled effectively by artillery on shore came to be regarded as the territorial sea under jurisdiction of the contiguous state. Beyond this delimited area the sea was common to all.

It became recognized as accepted international law that the maritime jurisdiction of a state terminated when its power of exercising continuous possession had been reached.[40]

Legal conceptions associated with freedom of the seas find acceptance with international jurists even though the juridical basis for the principle is divisible into the dichotomous theories of *res nullius* and *res communis*.[41]

Thus in 1926 the International Law Association, at its Vienna Conference, adopted the fundamental doctrine, Article I of the draft titled "Laws of Maritime Jurisdiction in Time of Peace," that "for the purpose of securing the fullest use of the seas, all States and their subjects shall enjoy absolute liberty and equality of navigation, transport, communications, industry, and science in and on the seas."[42]

Also, the Institute of International Law, after its Lausanne Conference in 1927, synthesized the modern legal position in a Declaration:

The principle of the freedom of the sea implies specially the following consequences:

(1) freedom of navigation on the high seas, subject to the exclusive control, in the absence of a convention to the contrary of the state whose flag is carried by the vessel;

(2) freedom of fisheries. . . ;

(3) freedom to lay submarine cables on the high seas; . . .[43]

It may be concluded that under general international law the high sea cannot be regarded as under the sovereignty of any state and that no state has a legal right to exercise jurisdiction over it.[44] But this broad statement fails to answer all of the multitudinous legal questions which are today arising, especially with respect to the rights of exploration, ownership, and juridical control of the resources of the oceans. These problems have been under study by international organizations since ocean potentials have been recognized, and attempts at codification of the law of the sea have ensued in the last four decades.

CHAPTER TWO

STUDY OF THE PROBLEM
BY INTERNATIONAL ORGANIZATIONS

THE LEAGUE OF NATIONS

EVOLUTIONARY ASPECTS of political and social influences from the Roman Empire through the turbulent years of dissonance among nations preceding and after World War I found culmination in the League of Nations, created as an international system for the maintenance of peace after the Armistice of November, 1918. The establishment of the League also led to the first worldwide endeavor to codify matters relevant to maritime law, particularly during periods of peace.[1]

CONVENTIONS SIGNED UNDER THE AUSPICES OF THE LEAGUE

Codification objectives pertaining to maritime law resulted in the insertion in Article 23 of the Covenant of the League that "subject to and in accordance with the provisions of international Conventions existing or hereafter to be agreed upon, the members of the League will make provision to secure and maintain freedom of communications and of transit and equitable treatment for the commerce of all members of the League." Thereafter, a conference met at Barcelona in

1921. There two conventions and statutes were formulated relative to "freedom of transit" and the "regime of navigable waterways of international concern."[2] There was a continuation of this codification in 1923 at the Geneva Conference. This conference was convened under the aegis of the League. An agreement was reached concerning the international regime of international ports.[3]

A further effort of codification was assumed by the League, with assistance from the Committee of Experts, composed of eminent jurisconsults. This committee had been commissioned to prepare a provisional list of significant topics for future deliberations concerned with feasible international regulation pertaining to topics to be included in the League's programme and a series of suggested priorities. The report submitted to the Assembly was considered in September, 1927.[4] The Assembly decision certified that a conference should be convened for the codification of pertinent topics, one of which was territorial waters.

The first international conference convened specifically to consider codification of international law met March 13 to April 12, 1930, at The Hague and was designated the Conference on the Progressive Codification of International Law. The conference failed to achieve concurrence concerning territorial waters, but a Draft Convention was prepared for future consideration regarding the legal status of the territorial sea.[5] The consideration of the breadth of the territorial sea together with rights of coastal states in contiguous waters was deemed to be one question rather than two. Conflicting and unreconcilable proposals concerning breadth of the territorial sea were propounded by various states. The Greek delegation, for example, was willing to accept a two-mile limitation if other delegates were in accord; a four-mile limitation was suggested by Norway and Sweden; six miles was agreeable to others.

A categorical concurrence to the proposition that there should be a uniform width for all considerations for all states had been the view of only a few states: Great Britain (South Africa, Australia, New Zealand, India), Italy, Japan, the Netherlands, and Poland. Opposition to this proposal was expressed by Belgium, Norway, and Sweden. Indecisive or unresponsive views were rendered by Germany, Estonia, France, Finland, Portugal, and the United States. That there should be acceptance of a uniform code and a maximum three-mile limitation for all purposes was the opinion of Great Britain, the Dominions, and Japan. Italy supported the six-mile limitation with specific rights beyond the six-mile zone. Both the Netherlands and Poland advocated certain variations from a maximum three-mile limitation.[6]

The rationale of state delegates was based upon various considerations, emphasizing divergent economic and geographical variants of coastal populations pertaining to freedom of navigation, national security, protection of neutrality in instances of armed hostilities, fisheries, customs regulations, traditional rights, and the inherent characteristics of the continental shelf.

Despite the wide disparity of opinions expressed by different governments concerning the breadth of the territorial sea, there was agreement relative to the topics to be considered at the forthcoming conference. Therefore, the Assembly of the League, following the report of the Experts Committee, agreed that three subjects be considered by the first conference, namely nationality, territorial waters, and the responsibility of states for damage caused in their territory to person or property of foreigners. Together with these topics, the matter of the exploitation of "the products of the sea" was deemed to be an appropriate topic for international consideration.[7]

The United Nations

CERTAIN BROAD RECOMMENDATIONS FOR UNITED NATIONS CONTROL

The League of Nations was, of course, superseded by the United Nations. A significant benefaction which was transmitted from the League to the United Nations was that at the termination of World War II the entire community of civilized nations gave approval to the establishment of the United Nations.[8]

Within the comprehensive framework of the United Nations it was logical that as an international institution it should direct attention to the accelerated international interest in oceanography, in the exploration and exploitation of the resources of the deep seas and the ocean floor. Responding to new technological competence which made available for exploitation the vast mineral resources of the oceans, organizations concerned with scientific, entrepreneurial, or governmental activities offered a plethora of resolutions. Recommendations were received from Monaco, Dakar, Geneva, London, New York, Rhode Island, from Bar Associations, United Nations Associations, parliamentarians, representatives from major governments.[9] There appears to be agreement concerning the four-point proposal relative to an ocean regime presented to the United Nations by Ambassador Arvid Pardo (Malta).[10] This proposal, which was initially made to the First Committee of the General Assembly on November 1, 1967, stated:

> Ocean space, beyond the limits of national jurisdiction, is the common heritage of mankind.
>
> Ocean space, beyond the limits of national jurisdiction, is not subject to claims of national sovereignty.
>
> Ocean space must be used for peaceful purposes only.
>
> The resources of ocean space, beyond the limits of national jurisdiction, must be explored and exploited with a maximum of international cooperation, for the benefit of all mankind.[11]

Despite basic agreement on these broad points, there are dilemmas inherent in them which are under examination by the Ad Hoc Committee, appointed by the 22nd General Assembly of the United Nations.

During 1968 two detailed draft treaties for the establishment of an ocean regime were published. Both draft treaties were structured on the Treaty on Outer Space which served only to provide a *code* concerning the activities of states.[12] It has been observed that an ocean treaty requires the creation of an institution to fulfill the myriad obligations to the sovereign nations of the world.[13] Such an institution would require the development of a code which would accommodate fluctuating technological advances and economic situations of nation-states and which might be called the ocean regime.[14]

Provisions in one treaty involve the extension of outer space law to ocean space, i.e., the freedom of exploration, cooperation, mutual assistance, mutual inspection, the status of vessels and installations. Prohibition of weapons of mass destruction is included, as are suggested relations to the United Nations, together with procedures for ratification. The terms of this treaty provide for the issuance of licenses for explorative operations and exploitation to either states or nongovernmental international organizations.[15] Both draft treaties fail to specify the composition of a stipulated supervisory agency.[16]

Until recent developments in marine science and technology, the new oceanic environment beyond the continental shelf has required no regulation. Extended exploration of the frontiers of oceanic depths will, however, present new problems. It may be logically assumed that in areas of this environment beyond national jurisdiction the

United Nations will be utilized for international consideration of oceanic problems, as it is an institution of multilateral and international responsibility.[17]

THE GENERAL ASSEMBLY

The General Assembly, a permanent body of the United Nations, is one of the six principal organs of the organization and is comprised of all the members. This body is regarded as a deliberative entity with broad powers of discussion, operating essentially as a forum for debate and recommendations within the scope of the Charter or relating to the organs of the United Nations.[18] Moreover, it possesses investigative powers, as well as capacity for review and supervision. It may criticize the work of the United Nations in its entirety, and of organs of the organization, including specialized agencies. However, its powers are limited; usually, adopted resolutions are interpreted as recommendations rather than as binding juridical decisions. The recommendations, although lacking legal authority, may serve to authorize action by member states.[19]

The General Assembly, in addition to its facultative or permissive competence, is given mandatory power for the initiation of studies. It may make recommendations for objectives which serve to encourage international cooperation concerning political issues as well as for promotion of codification and development of international law.[20] In this respect it serves the tradition of a quasi-legislative international institution. Powers of promoting the recommendations made by the General Assembly have significance as a political or moral influence and may acquire a legally binding status by consent, acquiescence, or by forms of estoppel.[21] It possesses an inherent right of *decision* only in substantive issues concerning internal affairs of the United Nations.

The General Assembly, through its quasi-parliamentary function, and pursuant to its obligation under Article 13 of the Charter, established on November 21, 1947, the International Law Commission. This commission presented a report to the General Assembly which included the legal regime of the high seas and territorial waters. Both these subjects were approved for presentation to the United Nations Conference on the Law of the Sea at the commission's Geneva session in July, 1956.[22] Significant conferences, which we shall consider in detail in Chapter 3, were also held in 1958 and 1960 at Geneva.

On December 28, 1967, at its twenty-second session,[23] the General Assembly, on the report of the First Committee,[24] adopted unanimously the following resolution on use of the seabed and ocean floor:

Examination of the question of the reservation exclusively for peaceful purposes of the seabed and the ocean floor, and the subsoil thereof, underlying the high seas beyond the limits of present national jurisdiction, and the use of their resources in the interests of mankind.

In this resolution the Assembly took cognizance of the fact that technological advancements in the field of oceanography had made the seabed, the ocean floor, and the subsoil thereof accessible for the exploitation of the resources of the sea for scientific, economic, military, and other purposes. These purposes will necessarily include geographical research in the heretofore inaccessible underwater world. It was therefore deemed essential to acquire definitive knowledge of oceanic topographical contours to make feasible the acquisition of the sea's limitless resources. The Assembly noted the magnitude of the geographical area of the sea, which constitutes almost two-thirds of the Earth's solid surface concealed from view beneath the waters of the oceans.[25] A significant portion of necessary research in the realm of oceanography must be accomplished not on land surfaces but at sea. The Assembly recognized the common interest of mankind in the ocean floor, and the opportunity afforded to the nations of the world community by the deep oceans for investigative purposes and for improved economic advantage in both living and nonliving resources.

Along these lines it is important to note the possibility and even probability of a new inhabitable continent under the seas, having towns, villages, farms, and industries exploiting the incalculable mineral resources of the ocean bed, which will be of great significance to the citizenry of the world community. Captain Jacques-Yves Cousteau, founder of the French Office for Undersea Research at Marseilles, is of the opinion that permanent stations for scientific purposes can be established beneath the sea at an estimated depth of at least 650 feet. These endeavors would represent the initial objectives in the eventual occupation of the underwater continental plateau by thousands of colonists, and would constitute realization of the conjectural ambitions of visionaries dating from the era of Alexander the Great. Such realization would greatly extend the area of human habitation on this overpopulated planet. Captain Cousteau has commented that it is the privilege of the present era to enter this vast unknown medium and to assess and exploit the natural resources of the oceans.[26] He further commented that actual residence for weeks and months of effective work in submarine areas will be accomplished in the actual colonization of the deeper ocean floor. His contribution to underwater explorations was enhanced by the organization of a scientific group *en mission* in the richest region of the oceans, the continental shelf, which contains petroleum, natural gas, sulfur, diamonds, and harvests for commercial fisheries. Still another probability of exploitation of the ocean areas is undersea stock farming—that is, the production of high-protein marine animals. These multiple activities in sea-floor industries must be consummated not from ships or towers but in actuality on the sea floor.[27]

Concerning the specific inclusion of the term "military" in the Assembly resolution, it may be said parenthetically that navies of certain nations are lending great support to modern research in oceanography; among such nations are Russia and the United States. The opacity of ocean waters being conducive to strategical maneuvers, defense purposes are served in the depths of ocean areas. The Assembly resolution included the provision that the exploration and utilization of the seabed, the ocean floor, and the subsoil should adhere to the principles and objectives of the Charter of the United Nations in the interest of the preservation of international peace and security for the benefit of mankind, and that detrimental uses of these areas would be opposed to the common interests of mankind. Therefore the Assembly sought the fosterage of international cooperative efforts and coordination in furthering peaceful exploration and use of oceanic areas.

The resolution took cognizance of previous and present significant work on allied questions concerning the sea carried forward by qualified entities of the United Nations, specialized agencies, the International Atomic Energy Agency, and other competent intergovernmental organizations.

Moreover, there was retrospective recognition of General Assembly Resolution 2172 and Economic and Social Council Resolution 1112 and the fact that surveys were being compiled by the secretary-general in response to these resolutions.

As a consequence of the above-mentioned resolutions, the General Assembly created a thirty-five-nation Ad Hoc Committee to study the peaceful utilization of the seabed and ocean floor beyond the territorial limits of national jurisdiction. The Ad Hoc Committee was requested to prepare, in cooperation with the secretary-general, a study for consideration by the General Assembly at its twenty-third session, which would include a survey of past and present activities of the United Nations, the specialized agencies, the International Atomic Energy Agency, and other intergovernmental bodies pertaining to the seabed and the ocean floor, and also of existing international agreements relative to these areas; an account of the scientific, technical, economic, and legal status of this topic; and to make suggestions concerning practical methods to encourage the promotion of international cooperation in the exploration, use, and conservation of the seabed, ocean floor, and the subsoil thereof, and indicating regard for the views and suggestions enunciated by member states during the deliberation of this item at the twenty-second session of the General Assembly.

The secretary-general was requested to transmit the text of the present resolution to the governments of all member states in order to ascertain their opinions regarding the subject. Records of the First Committee relative to the discussion of this item were requested for transmittal to the Ad Hoc Committee. Appropriate assistance was requested for the Ad Hoc Committee, including the rendering of results of studies undertaken as a consequence of General Assembly Resolution 2172 (XXI) and Economic and Social Resolution 1112 (XL) and such significant documentations concerning this item as may be prepared by the United Nations Educational, Scientific and Cultural Organization and its intergovernmental Oceanographic Commission, the Inter-governmental Maritime Consultative Organization, the Food and Agriculture Organization of the United Nations, the World Meteorological Organization, the World Health Organization, the International Atomic Energy Agency, and other intergovernmental entities.[28]

In conclusion, specialized agencies, the International Atomic Energy Agency, and other intergovernmental agencies were encouraged to cooperate with the Ad Hoc Committee in the fulfillment of the present resolution.[29]

THE UNITED NATIONS ECONOMIC AND SOCIAL COUNCIL

Under the Charter of the United Nations distributive powers and functions of the organization were vested in six different major organs, the third organ being the Economic and Social Council. This organ functions under the authority of the General Assembly. The Economic and Social Council was entrusted with the comprehensive objective of promoting economic and social progress among the nations of the world community, as a basis for the maintenance of peaceful and friendly relationships.[30]

The exploitation of natural resources of the sea is thus one of the primary concerns of the Economic and Social Council. In its debates on the subject it contemplated the conclusion of an ocean treaty calling for the creation of a Specialized Oceanic Agency, Authority, or Institution concerning the deep seas and ocean floor. The function of such an ocean agency or institution would be predominantly economic and scientific—with allocation of licenses for participants in the oceanic domain. The agency would, presumably, encourage and protect scientific research and development. It is anticipated that the governing body of this ocean agency will be elected by the Economic and Social Council.[31] Moreover, under the council's inclusive powers,[32] a resolution was adopted on March 7, 1966, requesting the secretary-general to make a survey of present knowledge concerning the resources of the sea beyond the continental shelves, and for the exploration of technological competence to exploit such resources of the sea.[33]

THE UNITED NATIONS INSTITUTE ON TRAINING AND RESEARCH

The General Assembly of the United Nations, in recognition of the interrelationship and interdependence existing between economic and social progress in the community of nations, requested the secretary-general to examine the feasibility of establishing a United Nations Institute on Training and Research to function under the aegis of the United Nations.[34] After study, there was established in March, 1965 the United Nations Institute of Training and Research (UNITAR). From its inception, the institute has emphasized coordination, especially with other United Nations institutes.

The executive director of the institute, in his report to the United Nations Second Committee, stated that many of the aspirations he had expressed in the twentieth session of the General Assembly were in the process of realization. His first report of UNITAR to the committee delineated intentions, while this current report was concerned with achievements. Specific research subjects were enumerated: development and modernization, studies in the area of international organization, and transnational studies relative to human rights and international law.[35]

The majority of delegations expressed approbation concerning UNITAR's accomplishments. The delegate of the Soviet Union, however, noted that a portion of the research program as well as some of the training activities which had previously been conducted by the United Nations had been diverted to UNITAR, after only informal discussions between officials of the two instrumentalities. The U.S.S.R. delegate objected to the change in status in both the training and research programs and insisted that such a transfer could be effected in the training program only after consultation with appropriate departments of the Secretariat and in the area of research, after a decision made by a qualified intergovernmental organization. He doubted the capacity of UNITAR to engage in research projects relative to maritime resources, since the subject was currently under deliberation by the intergovernmental Oceanographic Commission on UNESCO.[36]

The General Assembly thereupon recognized the necessity for increased knowledge of the oceans and of the opportunities available for the exploitation of living and nonliving resources within this domain.[37] The Assembly also noted the varied activities within the United Nations associated with the resources of the sea: the United Nations Educational, Scientific and Cultural Organization, and especially, its intergovernmental Oceanographic Commission; the Food and Agriculture Organization of the United Nations; its Committee on Fisheries; the World Meteorological Organization; the Advisory Committee on the Application of Science and Technology to Development; and other intergovernmental organizations, governments, universities, and scientific and technological institutions.[38]

The General Assembly therefore advocated endorsement of the Economic and Social resolution (1112 XL) of March 7, 1966, requesting that a survey be made by the secretary-general of the present knowledge of the resources of the sea beyond the continental shelf—excluding fisheries—together with current technical competence for the exploitation of these resources. The Assembly also requested the secretary-general to undertake cooperative participation with the above mentioned entities, beyond the survey requested by the Economic and Social Council, and to formulate proposals for the avoidance of duplicative endeavors. The secretary-general was encouraged to make effectual preparations for amplified international cooperation to aid, under the aegis of UNITAR, in the acquisition of more definitive knowledge of the marine environment through science and in the development and utilization of marine resources. The secretary-general was requested to initiate and to place emphasis upon marine education and training schedules, and to assemble a small group of experts, to be selected largely from the specialized agencies and appropriate intergovernmental organizations, to assist in the compilation of the inclusive survey. The Assembly then requested that the survey and proposals be submitted to the Advisory Committee on the Application of Science and Technology to Development for its consideration, and that the secretary-general present his survey and proposals, including comments by the Advisory Committee, to the General Assembly at its twenty-third session, through the Economic and Social Council.[39]

The vast operational aspects of UNITAR within the United Nations system can only be suggested. As an autonomous institute it has materially assisted in the solution of problems concerning other United Nations organizations which include political, economic, and social projects. Approximately seventy countries, as well as nongovernmental sources, have contributed voluntary financial support to UNITAR. Such support is indicative of the international commitment to its objectives.

The tasks undertaken by the institute include the distribution of technological data in conjunction with the United Nations Department of Economic and Social Affairs. These inclusive objectives are of paramount significance to the development of technological capability for the exploitation of the mineral resources of the ocean.[40] Still another subject to which the institute has directed attention is the development of natural resources. As an initial endeavor in this area, the institute plans the organization of a research seminar on the resources of the deep sea. This seminar will be conducted with the cooperation of the Department of Economic and Social Affairs. Its primary purpose will be to assemble on a selective basis an accredited group of recognized competence to consider the prospects of international cooperative efforts in the development of natural resources and of the deep sea.[41]

Finally, the institute is emphasizing codification and progressive development in international law. The preliminary studies will incorporate an empirical survey concerning the acceptance and impingement of major multilateral treaties such as the law of the sea, with special reference to the United Nations.[42] The United Nations Institute on Training and Research is urging clarification of the legal status governing the exploitation of mineral resources in the marine environment of the deep seabeds.[43]

THE INTERGOVERNMENTAL OCEANOGRAPHIC COMMISSION

Nation-states, international governmental organizations, nongovernmental participants, regional organizations, private entrepreneurs, advocates of enterprisory research and development programs, and scientists from many nations are engaged in various aspects of oceanography. The oceans offer a variety of opportunities for multi-users of the world, since benefits from the sea are innumerable.[44] All users and potential users share a common involvement in oceanic exploitation.

Because of the dependence of nations and individuals upon the world ocean for multiple reasons, the formulation of an adequate international oceanographic regime is imperative. Issues which are concomitant with the development of a feasible international regime for the oceans are further complicated by the long history through centuries of international, national, and private activities on the high seas.[45] Organizations associated with oceanic activities also have a complex history. The most universal international organization, the United Nations, has in given situations utilized its own vessels for special purposes.[46] A majority of the specialized agencies of the United Nations have involvements with some aspect of the ocean, as do other organizations with responsibilities in marine sciences. Subsidiary international groups, which include the specialized agency UNESCO, are participants in research and experimentation concerning the ocean or in the encouragement of international endeavors in this area. The Intergovernmental Conference on Oceanographic Research, convened in 1960, recommended the establishment of an intergovernmental oceanographic commission to function under the direction of and within the framework of UNESCO for the organization of concentrated action by states and by international entities. A primary objective was to promote interstate cooperation on a more permanent basis.[47]

At the beginning of the twentieth century, international scientific cooperation became significant on the occasion when Scandinavian countries joined together in the unified use of a single ship.[48] However, the first comprehensive multinational cooperative effort to investigate the oceans occurred as an important segment of the International Geophysical Year (IGY) under the aegis of the International Union of Geodesy and Geophysics in 1957. This successful venture preceded and encouraged the formation of the Special Committee on Oceanic Research (SCOR). The Special Committee, vitalized by the impetus acquired in international cooperation during the International Geophysical Year, organized a concerted study of the Indian Ocean.[49] Participants in the International Indian Ocean Expeditions represented twenty-three countries, with a total of 40 ships. There were 180 cruises during the period between 1959 and 1965. After that time, the nations recognized that cooperative oceanic endeavors necessitated a more formal consensual disposition or arrangement, to replace a nonintergovernmental group such as SCOR. Consequently, UNESCO established in 1960 the Intergovernmental Oceanographic Commission, which ultimately undertook the coordinative functions of SCOR for the Indian Ocean Expedition.[50] Other cooperative programs were inaugurated for study of other areas, including the tropical Atlantic, the Kuroshio Current off the coast of Japan, the Caribbean, and the Mediterranean. During the formative period, the commission was primarily concerned with the interchange of scientific data and international plans.[51] More recently its program has been extended beyond its original purposes to include diverse dilemmas associated with marine pollution, assistance to emerging nations, and legal phases of oceanic research and exploitation.[52]

Acting in a scientific advisory capacity to the Intergovernmental Oceanographic Commission, the Special Committee on Oceanic Research of the International Council of Scientific Unions also serves as the predominant coordinative functionary of the world's scientists.[53]

THE INTERNATIONAL LAW COMMISSION

As a consideration in the initial creation of the International Law

Commission it may be recalled that the governments participating in the drafting of the United Nations Charter were overwhelmingly opposed to the conferral of legislating power on the United Nations for the enactment of binding rules of international law. There was, however, obvious support for the conferral on the General Assembly of restricted powers of study and recommendation. This inclination directed adoption of the provision in Article 13, paragraph 1, which reads:

1. The General Assembly shall initiate studies and make recommendations for the purpose of:
a. . . .encouraging the progressive development of international law and its codification.[54]

In conformity with this directive, the General Assembly, during the second part of its first session on January 31, 1947, adopted Resolution 94 (1) providing for the establishment of the Committee on the Progressive Development of International Law and its Codification, the "Committee of Seventeen." The committee was requested to consider recommended procedures for discharging the General Assembly's responsibilities imposed under Article 13, paragraph 1.[55]

Following the establishment of the "Committee of Seventeen," the report was adopted which recommended the creation of an international law commission.

In 1950 the International Law Commission reviewed diverse questions which might be categorized under the general topic of the regime of the high seas; included in the list of questions so classified was that of the resources of the high seas and the continental shelf.[56]

At its third session in 1951, pursuant to a recommendation of the General Assembly of December 6, 1949, the International Law Commission decided to initiate consideration of the territorial sea. Also during 1951, the commission provisionally adopted draft resolutions relative to the continental shelf, the resources of the sea, and the contiguous zone.[57]

In 1953, at its fifth session, the International Law Commission reexamined the provisional draft articles and subsequently prepared final drafts on four questions: (1) the continental shelf; (2) resources of the sea; (3) sedentary fisheries; and (4) the contiguous zone. Following recommendations of the commission, the Assembly adopted a resolution which authorized the convening of an international conference of plenipotentiaries to "examine the law of the sea," including the legal, technical, economic, and political aspects of the subject, and to incorporate the results of its work in one or more international conventions.[58]

In conformity with the General Assembly resolution, the report of the International Law Commission was adopted in a formal conference as the foundation for the consideration of the law of the sea. Prior to the conference, comprehensive preparatory work was done by the commission, by delegations from respective governments, experts, members of the Sixth Committee, and many others. Culminating these concerted efforts, eighty-five states convened in Geneva from February 24 to April 27, 1958. The majority of the interested specialized agencies of the United Nations as well as intergovernmental bodies sent observers to the Conference on the Law of the Sea.[59]

In recapitulation it may be observed that international organizations, the League of Nations and its successor, the United Nations with its General Assembly, Economic and Social Council, Institute on Training and Research, and others are established instrumentalities to aid in the formulation of international, national, and regional legal regimes together with other policies pertaining to oceanography. As has been indicated, technological capability has made feasible the exploitation of oceanographic resources.[60]

The establishment of an oceanic regime appears to be imperative and should be based upon the fact that the ocean space is an indivisible ecological whole.[61] The problems associated with marine environment, marine science, economics, decision-making, and new domestic public law are to be considered in juxtaposition with jurisprudence.

It has been observed that through new policies concerning ocean-related activities, efforts have been made to develop international law; to seek the preservation of traditional freedom of the seas; to establish incentives for private investment; and to recognize the legitimacy of interests among all nations for ultimate benefits from that area of the deep ocean floor beyond national jurisdiction. In furtherance of such general policies there exists a combination of the elements of a pluralistic society which includes the innovative spirit of industry, the burgeoning knowledge of great universities, and the intricate processes of government.[62]

Presumably, the Economic and Social Council will be assigned still another duty in the coordination of concerted efforts of nations to formulate a multilateral treaty, similar in scope to the Outer Space Treaty, delineating a comprehensive oceanic regime of the law of the sea.

THE ORGANIZATION OF AMERICAN STATES

The Inter-American Council of Jurists and its permanent committee, the Inter-American Juridical Committee of Rio de Janeiro, began in 1950 a study of the "System of Territorial Waters and Related Questions." In 1953 at Buenos Aires, when the Inter-American Council of Jurists held its second meeting, it took cognizance of the committee report but asked for continuation of the study under consideration and for the subsequent submission of a more detailed report. In 1954, at the suggestion of the delegation of Ecuador at the Tenth Inter-American Conference at Caracas, it was agreed that a specialized conference was to be convened with the objective of studying the judicial and economic system relative to the submarine shelf, oceanic waters, and their natural resources in the light of contemporary knowledge.[63] Also, the Caracas conference made certain analogous declarations concerning substantive aspects of the subject.

At the Caracas conference, competent inter-American bodies, including the Inter-American Council of Jurists, were empowered by a resolution to assist in the preparatory work for the Specialized Conference.[64] Pursuant to this objective, the subject "System of Territorial Waters and Related Questions" was placed on the agenda of the third meeting of the Inter-American Council of Jurists, which was convened in 1956 in Mexico City. Resolution XIII was adopted, to the effect that the council "recognizes as the expression of the Juridical conscience of the Continent," that "each State is competent to establish its territorial waters within reasonable limits, taking into account geographical, geological, . . . as well as the economic needs of its population, and its security and defense."[65] From the initial discussions of organized community considerations, among the American states as well as in the International Law Commission, there was consensus that coastal states were, or should be, entitled to exercise exclusive control over vertical and horizontal exploitative operations for offshore mineral resources.

Although the Inter-American Specialized Conference which convened at Ciudad Trujillo, Dominican Republic, on March 15-23, 1956, was characterized by absence of agreement upon many other issues, it affirmed the exclusive rights of the coastal state for exploitation of offshore mineral resources.[66]

In concurrence with the resolution at the Tenth Inter-American Conference, the Specialized Conference examined in their entirety various aspects of the juridical-economic system applicable to the submarine shelf and oceanic waters, together with ascertainable resources acknowledged in current scientific data.[67] However, only one issue, that of the rights of the contiguous state to exploit the resources of the seabed and subsoil of the continental shelf, was affirmatively concluded. The relevant portion of the affirmed resolution stated:

1. The seabed and subsoil of the continental shelf, continental and insular terrace, or other submarine areas, adjacent to the coastal state, outside the area of the territorial sea, and to a depth of 200 meters or, beyond that limit, to where the depth of the superjacent waters admits of the exploitation of the natural resources of the seabed and subsoil, appertain exclusively to that state and are subject to its jurisdiction and control.[68]

Concerning additional topics on the agenda of the conference (juridical regime of the waters above the submarine areas, the question of determining whether given living resources attach to the seabed or to the superjacent waters, conservation of the living resources of the high seas, the breadth of the territorial sea), attention was directed to the lack of agreement and the diversity of opinions existing among American states. The conference refrained from stating a position on these questions but recommended continued diligence in efforts to achieve acceptable solutions.[69]

The Resolution of Ciudad Trujillo approved by the Inter-American Specialized Conference was titled, "Conservation of Natural Resources: The Continental Shelf and Marine Waters."

Brazil abstained from stating a position on possible solutions. Regarding the Resolution of Ciudad Trujillo and matters of disagreement, Mexico stated:

1. There is no general rule in international law setting the extent of the territorial sea.

2. Each state has the right to set the extent of its territorial sea within reasonable limits, taking into consideration both the pertinent geographical, geological,

biological, economic, and social factors, and the needs of security and defense.[70]

The Delegation of El Salvador voted affirmatively on the Resolution of Ciudad Trujillo because the document did not prejudice the rights of El Salvador to the continental terrace adjacent to its coast or to its territorial sea, which according to El Salvador extends to a distance of two hundred nautical miles measured from the low-water line, without affecting the freedom of navigation accepted by principles of international law.[71]

The United States of America, among other statements and reservations, declared its position: "The Government of the United States does not recognize that a state has competence to determine the breadth of its territorial sea apart from international law."[72]

The United States representative at the sessions of Committee I opposed and voted against the Resolution on Territorial Waters and Related Questions. In the recorded rationale it was stated that the Inter-American Council of Jurists had lacked the benefit of essential analytical studies prepared by its permanent committee, which the jurists had consistently regarded as of inestimable significance in the formulation of acceptable conclusions concerning the issues involved; that at this meeting of the Council of Jurists there had been substantially no discussion or serious consideration of important implications in the resolution; that the resolution included pronouncements founded upon economic and scientific assumptions which were unsubstantiated in factual data and which were properly within the competence of the Specialized Conference under the terms of the Resolution of the Tenth Inter-American Conference; and that a portion of the resolution was in opposition to international law. The representative further stated that the resolution ignored the interests and rights of states other than the adjacent coastal states in both the conservation and utilization of marine resources, and that it ignored as well the acknowledged necessity for international cooperative efforts to achieve common objectives; further, that the resolution served political objectives and in this exceeded the competence of the Council of Jurists as a technical juridical entity.[73]

Finally, the United States delegation protested that in the drafting of the resolution, in which the United States lacked participation and had not been recognized when the issue was submitted to Committee

I, there had been no discussions of the position of the United States and other delegations at the only session called by the committee to discuss the document.[74]

The delegations of Costa Rica, Chile, Ecuador, and Peru declared that their endorsement of the resolutions, agreements, and recommendations adopted at the Ciudad Trujillo Conference and contained in the Resolution of Ciudad Trujillo did not change in any manner their constitutional provisions, their national legislative enactments, their multilateral agreements, or their collective international documents concerning the subject.[75]

Thus, while delegations from various nations expressed diverse views concerning issues presented for consideration to the Ciudad Trujillo Conference, unanimity was achieved concerning the right of the coastal state to the exclusive exploitation of the mineral resources of the seabed.

CHAPTER THREE

DEVELOPMENT AND CODIFICATION OF THE LAW OF THE SEA

INTRODUCTION

CUSTOMARY OR TRADITIONAL INTERNATIONAL LAW took cognizance of the division of the sea into two domains only: the territorial sea, which included internal waters, and the high seas.[1] The sovereignty of the coastal state was the predominant principle of the regime of the territorial sea, while the regime of the high seas recognized the principle of the freedom of the seas, which included the right of all states to utilize and exploit its marine resources.

Polemical issues antedating the *Mare Liberum* and *Mare Clausum* dictum, previously mentioned, existed in the sixteenth and seventeenth centuries. At the beginning of the sixteenth century, Spanish jurists and theologians (especially Francisco Alfonso de Castro, Fernando Vazquez de Menchaca, and Francisco de Vitoria) enunciated the doctrine of the high seas, impugning the right of a nation to exercise sovereignty over the seas and its waters. Donellus and Gentilis reanimated the concept of the Roman *jus gentium*, elevating the doctrine into international status.[2] It may also be recalled that in regard to the juridical nature of the high seas, the doctrine of *res nullius* and *res*

33

communis had been debated by jurists. Grotius and his predecessors supported, as previously indicated, the doctrine of *res communis* and therefore regarded the sea as incapable of effective occupation.[3] The juridical dilemma, continuing during intervening centuries, was presented for consideration at The Hague in 1925 during the session of the Institute of International Law. No definitive conclusion was reached, but the consensus was in support of the thesis that the sea might properly be categorized as *res communis*.[4] Subsequent opinions seem to indicate that the high seas may not be appropriated by any state, nor does the international community possess an inherent right to sovereignty of the high seas, since all states have an equal right in the "use" of the high seas.[5]

The doctrine of the freedom of the seas is based upon the dual purposes served by the sea—as a recognized means of communication and as a source of wealth.[6] The principle of the freedom of the seas is applicable to navigation, to commerce, and to the use and exploitation of the resources of the sea.

Prior to the 1930 Conference at The Hague, it should be recalled, Article 23 of the Covenant of the League of Nations provided:

Subject to and in accordance with the provisions of international Conventions existing or hereafter to be agreed upon, the Members of the League will make provision to secure and maintain freedom of communications and of transit and equitable treatment for commerce of all members of the League.

Thereafter in 1921 a conference met in Barcelona. Two conventions were concluded relative to "freedom of transit" and "the regime of navigable waterways of international concern." The codification was continued at the Geneva Conference of 1923.[7]

THE 1930 CONFERENCE AT THE HAGUE

Following the conferences of 1921 and 1923, conventions were signed under the auspices of the League of Nations in 1930 at The Hague. The resources of the sea environment were referred to as a "common patrimony."[8] The first Conference on the Progressive Codification of International Law was assembled at The Hague on March 13–April 12, 1930. Forty-two states sent delegates, and others sent observers.

One of the three subjects placed on the agenda of the conference was the regime of the territorial sea. Although diversity of opinion prevented concurrence on the breadth to be allocated to this area of the sea, the conference established a foundational structure of concepts and principles which were subsequently incorporated into the international law of the sea.[9]

The Hague Conference of 1930 was given significant assistance in its efforts toward codification by the Committee of Experts. In September, 1927, after the committee's report was submitted to the Assembly, the decision was made to convene a conference to codify three subjects, of which only one, territorial waters, is of relevance here. The accomplishment of this conference was confined to the preparation of a draft convention on "The Legal Status of the Territorial Sea," to be used for subsequent deliberation and recommendations. Also, there was adopted a resolution on the territorial sea, to which thirteen articles were annexed dealing with its legal status. Through replies to the "Questionnaire" prepared by the Codification Committee, official views of respective governments were recorded. The paramount difficulties in arriving at agreement were associated with (1) the breadth of the territorial sea; (2) the right of a state to take measures outside this breadth in an adjacent and contiguous area; and (3) the definition of the nature of the rights which states are entitled to exercise over the territorial sea.[10]

The Assembly of the League, in concurrence with the report of the Experts' Committee, concluded that "the question of the exploitation of the products of the sea" was an appropriate topic for international agreement. However, little more was done by the League on this matter.

In Article 13 of the Charter of the United Nations the General Assembly was charged with the explicit obligation to initiate studies and to make recommendations which would serve to promote the "progressive development of international law and its codification." Pursuant to this directive, the International Law Commission was established November 21, 1947.[11]

A substantive portion of each of the commission's reports was related to the legal regimes of the high seas and of territorial waters. At the commission's eighth session at Geneva in July, 1956, the subjects were approved for presentation to the United Nations Conference on the Law of the Sea.[12]

The 1958 and 1960 Conferences at Geneva

The 1958 and 1960 conferences at Geneva were preceded by consideration of the regime of the territorial sea by the International Law Commission, which had included the question in its agenda since its fourth session in 1952.[13]

In April, 1953, a group of experts composed of various governments held a meeting at The Hague with the Special Rapporteur serving as chairman of the group. In 1954 the Special Rapporteur, in his third report concerning the regime of the territorial sea, included opinions received from governments, their observations, and practice regarding delimitation zones of two adjacent states. These observations were reflected in changes at the eighth session of the commission, when the final draft on the territorial sea was submitted.[14]

At the commission's sixth and seventh sessions during 1954 and 1955 the provisional articles relative to the regime of the territorial sea were adopted.

In 1955, following the General Assembly Resolution 899 (IX) of December 14, 1954, the commission adopted at its seventh session a provisional draft on the regime of the high seas, based upon the sixth report of the Special Rapporteur. At its eighth session in 1956, the commission made a final report on subjects pertinent to the high seas. Also, draft provisions concerning the law of the sea were revised by the commission to encompass a composite body of rules.[15]

The final report on the law of the sea, which included seventy-three articles and commentaries, was submitted to the General Assembly in 1956. The Assembly by Resolution 1105 (XI) of February 21, 1957, authorized the convening of an international conference of plenipotentiaries

to examine the law of the sea, taking account not only of the legal but also of the technical, economic, and biological aspects of the problem, and to embody the results of its work in one or more international conventions or such other instruments as the conference may deem appropriate.[16]

The final report of the commission constituted the basis for conference consideration of the many-faceted problems which were inseparable from the development and codification of the law of the sea. Together with the final report, the conference had additional data of more than thirty preliminary documents from the United Nations Secretariat, specialized agencies, and various independent experts which were prepared in response to an extended invitation of the secretary-general to introduce specialized subjects.[17]

The conference created five primary committees: First Committee (territorial sea and contiguous zone); Second Committee (high seas: general regime); Third Committee (high seas: fishing and conservation of living resources); Fourth Committee (continental shelf); and Fifth Committee (question of free access to the sea of landlocked countries). These committees presented a résumé report of their work with appended draft articles to the plenary meeting of the conference. It was agreed that the draft articles and amendments would be embodied in four separate conventions: the Convention on the Territorial Sea and Contiguous Zone; the Convention on the High Seas; the Convention on Fishing and Conservation of the Living Resources of the High Seas; and the Convention on the Continental Shelf. The Fifth Committee recommendations were included in Article 14 of the Convention on the Territorial Sea and the Contiguous Zone and in Articles 2, 3, and 4 of the Convention on the High Seas. Each convention was to become effective thirty days after twenty-two accessions were submitted to the secretary-general of the United Nations.[18]

By Resolution 1307 (XIII), the General Assembly on December 10, 1958, authorized the secretary-general to convene a second Conference on the Law of the Sea to reconsider the issues concerning (1) delimitation of the territorial sea and (2) fishery limits, left undetermined by the first Conference on the Law of the Sea. In conformity with this authorization, the Second Conference convened in Geneva from March 17 to April 27, 1960, with representatives of eighty-eight states in attendance.[19]

Once again, no substantive decisions on the two questions were consummated, yet the conference acquired some indicia of international agreement as criteria for further consideration.

Despite the failure to achieve concurrence on these two subjects, the United Nations Conference on the Law of the Sea is indubitably the most significant international conference convened to consider them, as well as one of the most important efforts ever devised by governments to codify international law.[20]

Even though all of the conventions were not immediately ratified by a majority of participating states or by twenty-two states whose

signatures were essential to achieve binding effect, the adoption of
the four conventions by a substantial majority represented the most
recent enunciation of the law on the subject considered.[21] Thus, the
General Conferences of 1958 and 1960 may be regarded as a substantive contribution to the eventual codification of the law of the sea.
These conventions have achieved a recognized status in contemporary
international law. As an example, in the case of *Arctic Maid Fisheries
Inc. et al.* v. *State of Alaska* the Supreme Court of Alaska took note of
a letter from the State Department in which the observation was made
in substance that although the Convention on Fishing and Conservation of the Living Resources of the High Seas is not in force because
twenty-two states had not yet acceded to it, its adoption by a substantial majority of the states of the world constituted the best indication of current international law on the subject. Also, in the case of
Re Dominion Coal Company Ltd. the Supreme Court of Nova Scotia
considered the terms of the same convention (Article 7) to ascertain
whether Spanish Bay was to be regarded as internal or territorial
waters.[22]

CONVENTION ON THE CONTINENTAL SHELF

Initial formulations of the "doctrine of the continental shelf" were
associated with scientific and economic interests. The Spanish ocean-
ographer Odon de Buen presented the thesis in 1918 at the National
Conference on Fisheries (Madrid) that although the domain of the
ocean should appertain to all users, the continental shelf should be
regarded as an extension or continuation of the coast of the adjoining
nation, since the land exercised a greater influence on this area than
the sea.[23] Mid-twentieth century discussions concerning the continental
shelf resulted in similar international attention. While it had limited
emphasis at an earlier date, the Treaty between the United Kingdom
and Venezuela (of February 26, 1942, relative to the submarine areas
of the Gulf of Paria) was the initial instrument in this geographical
area. Following this proclamation, other countries issued decrees and
declarations.[24]

Since technological competence has made feasible the exploitation
of minerals deposited in the subsoil of the continental shelf, questions
arise concerning installations erected in or beneath or above the sea
for the extraction of petroleum and other minerals. Such installations

are obstructions to navigation, especially when numerous objects are situated in one area (as derricks for offshore drilling operations) and in locations frequented by shipping enterprises. In instances where installations are being constructed beyond the territorial waters of a particular state, the issue involves the inquiry as to whether the rights accure to any given state or only to the coastal state.[25]

Definition of the Continental Shelf

Much disparity exists between the geological-geographical conception of the continental shelf and the juridical definition contained in the Geneva Convention of 1958. The continental shelf is the submerged bed of the sea and is actually appurtenant to a contiguous continental land mass.

At least a limited knowledge of oceanographical, geological, and geographical aspects of the topography of the shelf is essential if one is to define the complex term *continental shelf*. Numerous soundings made by scientists engaged in oceanic explorative expeditions have revealed topographical variance in submarine areas adjacent to coastal states. The soundings indicated that from the shore the depth of the sea increased gradually to an average depth of two hundred meters. Beyond the two-hundred-meter dimension the depth of the sea increased; the isobath of approximately two hundred meters comprised an edge or border of the area.[26] Many slopes are incised with steep-walled canyons caused by turbidity currents. The margins of the continents vary in length and width. These margins were given identity in 1887 by Hugh Robert Mill, who called them continental shelves. The declivity from the outer edge of the continental shelf, the submerged portion existing between the shelf and the ocean-bottom, is the continental slope. Contiguous to the continental slope and connecting it to the land is the continental shelf. This zone of shallow water, notable for its disparity of dimensions in various localities, is of major significance for economic considerations. An additional geological phenomenon of the continental shelf is the lack of structural uniformity on the surface of the area. There are geomorphological features known as submarine canyons which originate in steep, narrow gorges. The canyons traverse the continental shelf for some twelve kilometers and proceed down the continental slope to vast depths. At the borderline of the shelf the bottom may be several hundred to a thousand meters below the adjacent sea floor.[27] The topographical irregularities on the shelves of many nations consist of submarine canyons, furrows, hills, trenches, troughs, and hollows. In formerly glaciated coasts the shelf is described as wide and deep and as having an irregular surface. Also, in localities of active coral growth the shelves are shallow and have irregular shoals and banks.[28] Because of existing variance in topographical submarine areas, it is obvious that efforts to delimit the continental shelf will encounter difficulty.

Principal Issues

The term *continental shelf* may be defined by geologists, geographers, and other scientists as the submarine extension of the given continent onward into the sea; or it may be regarded as a foundational structure for the support of the superstructure of continents. The shelf lies between the terrestrial shoreline and the first substantial declivity on the seaward side, without regard to its depth. This submarine plain borders all the continents. Since the plain varies in width, areas of it have been categorized as "inner" shelf and "outer" shelf, "continental" shelf and "insular" shelf, "real" shelf and "false" shelf.[29]

Other considerations involve the fact that the earth, momentarily considered as isolated from the vast water impediment covering 70 percent of its surface (hydrosphere), has on its terrestrial crust (lithosphere) two paramount geographical components: (1) the continents and their continental shelves, and (2) the deep ocean basins with steep sloping sides designated as continental slopes.[30] Five continents (North America, South America, Europe-Asia, Africa, Australia) are circumscribed by a single belt of shallow water, an almost continuous continental shelf of irregular widths. Configurations vary in oceanic areas, those of the Pacific, Atlantic, and Indian Oceans. The total area of the five mentioned continents and the sixth continent of Antarctica together with their respective continental shelves would approximate 68,500,000 square miles. The continental shelves, including insular shelves, may be estimated at 10,500,000 square miles, or approximately 7.6 percent of the total ocean area of the world.[31] The continental shelves approximate one-fifth of the land area of the world; the deep ocean basins are perhaps twelve times the area of the continental shelves.

Continental shelves are regarded as *outward extensions* of the continents having relatively shallow waters which drop sharply to continental slopes and, in many instances, into the ocean basins at the two-hundred-meter depth. In specific localities off the coast of South America, particularly off the Peruvian, Ecuadorian, and Chilean coastal areas, and off the coast of east Africa, there is a negligible continental shelf. The steep ocean basin edges are situated almost at the shore line. The existence of this geological factor has produced legal dilemmas associated with the inordinate claims to sovereignty over the high seas asserted by South American countries, especially Peru, Ecuador, and Chile.[32] Legal postulates presented in justification of claims made by states to the resources of their continental shelves should include a consideration of geological data supporting the fact that the continental shelves are a definite continuation of the continent. Therefore, the term *continuity* is applicable to the continental shelves, as they are actually an integral part of continents, not merely contiguous to the continents.[33]

Still another issue arises from the great variation in the widths of the respective continental shelves. The mean width for continental shelves of the world has been estimated at thirty miles, but this calculation is based on numerical figures of zero to more than eight hundred miles. To compensate for the geographical lack of continental shelves, certain states with limited continental shelves, or none at all, have made excessive claims to the resources of the high seas contiguous to their coastlines.[34]

The lack of uniformity in depth of the edge of the continental shelf presents additional issues. The edge is usually regarded as the line where the depth reaches two hundred meters, or the hundred-fathom line; yet there is a variance from less than one hundred meters to more than four hundred meters.[35] The continental shelf was delimited by the Geneva Convention on the Continental Shelf, in terms of a two-hundred-meter depth; but it could include an area beyond this limit to the depth of the superjacent waters when the depth permits the exploitation of the national resources of these areas.[36] The shelf is a submerged border of the continental crust, and in some instances the shelf may be virtually nonexistent. In areas off glaciated coasts near the origin of large rivers, and in localities with broad lowlands, the shelf may be exceedingly wide. Established seismic and deep sounding measurements indicate that bottom configurations vary greatly in different oceanic areas. In many regions such as the North Polar Sea and the South Indian and South Pacific Oceans, observations are limited because of inadequate topographical knowledge and will require intensive national and international cooperative efforts.[37]

Subsequent State Practice:
Claims to the Continental Shelf Resources

Centuries ago the first claims were made to certain resources of the sea in the area now designated as the seabed of the continental shelf. It has been said that such claims were made as early as the sixth century b.c.[38]

Fulton maintains that the coral and pearl fisheries may be regarded as belonging to the soil or bed of the sea rather than to the sea itself. This principle is recognized in municipal law, and international law also recognizes a claim in given instances to such fisheries when they exist on submarine soil beyond the usual territorial limit. Pearl fisheries have been regarded from time immemorial as proper subjects of both property claims and jurisdiction. Coral beds in the Mediterranean, adjacent to the coasts of Algeria, Sardinia, and Sicily, were similarly regulated beyond the three-mile limit by Italian and French laws.[39] Philip C. Jessup cited an Indian case in which chank beds located five miles from the Ramnad coast were regulated. The history of the Ceylon chank fisheries extended from the sixth century b.c. to modern periods. The rationale of the court in this case was that since the Ramnad proprietor had by claim held the chank beds by immemorial privilege, he had a possessory property right in the chanks. The case was decided upon the dictum of the immemorial claim of the land sovereign over particular waters.[40]

In the eighteenth century Vattel asserted that the uses of the sea adjacent to the coast rendered it subject to appropriation because it provided shells, pearls, and other commodities. A maritime people might, in his view, rightfully appropriate and convert the products of the sea to their own advantage as an appendage to the land which they occupied.[41]

One of the first legislative acts in the nineteenth century concerning continental shelf resources was the British Colonial Act of 1811, in which the British claimed exclusive control over the seabed resources (sedentary fisheries). This act declared dominion over the Ceylon pearl banks in an area far in excess of the three-mile limit. On subsequent dates similar legislative acts were published by the British Colonial Office.

During the late nineteenth century, from 1881 to 1898, Australia enacted legislation for protective and regulatory measures concerning sedentary fisheries. The enactment gave the coastal state control over a wide area of the high sea far beyond territorial waters. For more than a century certain states have issued regulations regarding seabed resources beyond territorial waters (i.e., sedentary fisheries). For centuries some of the resources of the seabed both within and extending beyond the coastal states' territorial sea have been subject to limited control and exploitation. Historically, states have recognized the exclusive rights of the coastal state over resources of sedentary fisheries of the seabed extending seaward beyond territorial waters, especially when effective and continuous use has been exercised by the coastal state.[42] Continued recognition of this right to the sedimentary fish on the continental shelf is enunciated in the Geneva Convention on the Continental Shelf. Therefore, it seems indisputable that the sovereignty of the coastal state includes the right to legislate concerning activities taking place on the surface of or under the seabed, such as dredging or oyster and sponge fisheries. Mining operations may also extend from land to below the low water mark. The only limitation binding upon the legislative power is that it shall not obstruct the right of innocent passage.[43] It may be assumed that legal difficulties emerging from conflicting claims to seabed resources beyond the environment of territorial waters have been inconsequential and have usually been resolved by legislative enactments or by treaty.

In English law it is asserted that the Crown is owner of the land area beneath the territorial sea. British legislation extended Britain's regulation of oyster beds more than twenty miles from its land territory into the St. George Channel and pearl fisheries in the Gulf of Manaar, located between India and Ceylon. There was also formal recognition by Great Britain that the Tunisian government had exclusive jurisdiction over the sponge fisheries beyond its territorial limits. Still other claims have been made by Mexico, Colombia, and others. Technical progress has made feasible the drilling of petroleum wells in shallow waters such as those situated off the coast of Mexico and also in the Persian Gulf. If these operations are beyond the territorial limits, they must necessarily be considered as an occupation of the seabed.[44]

Although claims of states to seabed resources on the continental shelf have been put forth for centuries, claims by states to the subsoil resources of the shelf are of more recent derivation.[45] The initial claim in this area was made more than a century ago in England when on August 2, 1858, royal approval was granted to an act called the Cornwall Submarine Mines Act, which promulgated the dictum that all mines and minerals below low water mark under the open sea, adjacent to but not constituting part of the County of Cornwall, were, as between the Queen and the Duke of Cornwall, vested in the Queen as composing part of the territorial possessions of the Crown.[46]

Additional underseas mining operations, particularly of coal, stimulated nineteenth-century claims by various states to subsoil resources of the continental shelves. Frequently the claims were within territorial waters of the littoral state. Claims were made by Australia, Chile, Japan, and Canada; and other English claims were made in addition to the Cornwall mines' claim. These claims were supported by the recognized right of a coastal state to exploit and occupy the subsoil under the high seas by extending mining installations from entrances situated on the territory of the coastal state or in its territorial waters.[47] The exploitation of minerals was achieved by the utilization of tunnels based on the landmass. A difference in terminology exists between nineteenth-century claims and antecedent claims concerning the continental shelf. The term *continental shelf* had not yet come into common usage in the nineteenth century. Twentieth-century claims, however, usually employ the term.

The exploitation of the continental shelves in the twentieth century has generally been for petroleum products. This often necessitates the construction of installations permanently attached to the seabed and the subsoil of the shelf or on stabilized platforms. These installations are erected above the surface of the high seas, and such projections obviously interfere with the free use of portions of the sea by other states for such purposes as navigation, fishing, depositing and maintenance of cable and pipe lines, and scientific research.[48]

Because of the possibility of unjustifiable interference by the littoral state through its exploitation of the continental shelf with the unencumbered use of the sea by other states, the draft articles of the

International Law Commission and the Geneva Convention on the Continental Shelf (1958) incorporated provisions prohibiting unjustifiable interference.[49] Because of technological deficiencies in exploration and exploitation of the resources of the seabed and subsoil, nineteenth-century claims, like earlier ones, did not result in interference with the freedom of the seas, since methods of exploitation did not involve installations in the high seas. Sedentary fisheries were necessarily harvested by ships; mineral exploitations were accomplished by a tunnel located on the landmass.

The Geneva Convention on the Continental Shelf marked the culmination of a tendency, first expressed in 1945-49 in a series of unilateral declarations, of maritime states to assert claims to exclusive jurisdiction or control over certain resources of the continental shelf and offshore locations. Justification for these claims was dependent upon factual data involving geographical contiguity and national security. Initially the objective was the reservation to littoral states of such oil as might be extractable from shelf areas, yet the claims were expressed in such broad terms as to include all mineral and even non-mineral resources.[50]

CONVENTION ON THE TERRITORIAL SEA AND THE CONTIGUOUS ZONE

Customary rules of international law concerning the territorial sea and the contiguous zone have been enunciated through controversial, divergent opinions and practices of nations extending over a period of approximately two centuries. The nature of the jurisdiction within this area and the extent of the territorial sea have evoked comment from ancient and modern juridical authorities.

The regime of the sea was not recognized by ancient Greece and Rome, for they dominated the sea by prowess, using it to serve economic and political needs. Moreover, there is no evidence to support a legal concept of maritime dominion in the Middle East and other areas in ancient times. Thus, historical data concerning international relations during remote historical periods yield only meager information as to origins of the juridical concepts of the sea. Jurists of ancient Rome described the sea as *res nullius,* ascribing ownership to the initial effective occupant.[51] Justinian set forth the dictum in his *Institutes* that the sea and its shorelines belong to all men, and are, therefore, open to public use. This doctrine was inseparable from the principle of *jus gentium* and consequently was inapplicable to international concepts of the free use of the sea, since an opposing theory of *Mare Nostrum* involving territorial sovereignty over the entire sea was accepted. The concept of *Mare Nostrum* recognized no belt or margin of sea adjacent to the coastal state. Such a marine zone emerged subsequently when certain medieval sovereigns and cities laid special claim to designated areas of the sea contiguous to their states' sovereign territorial boundaries.[52]

Since the regime applicable to the exploitation and conservation of the mineral resources of the sea is dependent upon the juridical nature of the portion of the sea in which the resources are to be found, customary international law must rationalize diverse national interests by equitable and feasible solutions regarding the territorial sea (including territorial waters) and the open sea areas. As we have previously indicated, technological sophistication and economic and social demands have resulted in extensions of state competence into areas which were formerly controlled by the regime of the open seas. It is, therefore, essential to consider the juridical nature of the various subdivisions of the sea, since state competence has been extended and exercised in different sea areas. Prior to the beginning of the twentieth century, a consensus existed concerning the breadth of the territorial sea. However, a change then occurred which is attributable to diversity of practice among coastal states. Because of the multiple rights which contiguous states may exercise in this territorial maritime zone according to present-day international legal concepts, the question is inextricable from the general juridical system controlling the sea.[53]

Of the vast oceanic areas of the globe only a negligible portion lies within the national jurisdiction of independent states. The portions which are under the national jurisdiction of the respective countries include all the fresh water and many landlocked areas of salt water, together with the territorial margins; the remainder exists beyond the national jurisdiction of any given state. Waters outside national jurisdiction have been governed for centuries by legal codes which were acceptable to civilized nations and which were incorporated within the body of laws called international law or the law of nations.[54] By general agreement navigable waters are categorized as "internal waters," "territorial waters," and the "high seas." All water areas, both salt and fresh, which are situated within the base line of territorial waters are commonly included under the generic term *internal waters*. These waters include all rivers, fresh water lakes, water within ports, and other landlocked waters. The state has unequivocal sovereignty over these waters. Territorial waters reach seaward from their base line to the extent of three nautical miles, although some states make more extensive, even exaggerated, claims.[55]

The territorial margin or belt constitutes part of the national domain of the state, as it is a prolongation of its territory, and is under its unlimited territorial jurisdiction. This area differs from internal waters since the belt carries an international responsibility for innocent passage for foreign merchant ships, particularly in time of peace.[56]

Each sovereign state may exercise unlimited territorial jurisdiction within its own territorial boundaries, subject only to such limitations as may be established by international customary laws, treaties, and general legal principles recognized by civilized nations. Limitations on territorial jurisdiction must be unequivocally established. States generally exercise authority to "reserve all resources of the territorial sea to exclusive national exploitation."[57] Mutual recognition of state sovereignty imposes a legal duty to observe the territorial jurisdiction of other states.[58] Axiomatically there is recognition of the division of the major land areas of the earth among sovereign states, as well as a margin of territorial sea adjacent thereto, together with the subsoil beneath and the airspace above. Individual states are prohibited by international law from appropriating the high seas and may not, therefore, claim territorial jurisdiction over the area.[59] All states, however, possess equality of right to "use" the high seas. From this vantage point the principle of the freedom of the seas may be formulated. This approach is removed from the concept of condominium, of community of property, and is attached to the right of use by all states beyond the limits of the sea reserved for each state. Within this precept, it is only necessary to determine with a degree of exactitude the meaning of the right. The doctrine of the freedom of the seas has its inception in the dual means of utilization of the sea—as a medium of communication and as a primary source of wealth. Therefore, since its formulation the principle has been regarded as applicable to navigation and commerce, as well as to the use and exploitation of the natural resources of the sea.

Hence, the concept of the sea as a medium of communication and as a source of wealth has prevailed in the doctrine of the freedom of the seas in international law.[60] The principle of *res communis,* that is, equality of rights for all states to utilize and exploit the resources of the seas, includes any form of use or exploitation afforded by the particular area of the sea.[61]

As has been previously indicated, the International Law Commission, pursuant to efforts initiated in 1930 to direct attention to the codification of the law of the sea, also set forth provisions for the sovereignty of the coastal state and for the competency to designate regulatory measures for observance by vessels in the territorial sea.[62]

The Convention on the Territorial Sea and the Contiguous Zone contains thirty-two articles. Concerning the territorial sea, the convention provides that the sovereignty of a given state extends beyond its territorial domain and its internal waters, to a margin of sea contiguous to its coast which is designated as the territorial sea. Sovereignty over this area is exerted subject to stipulations contained within these articles as well as to additional precepts of international criteria. The sovereignty of a littoral state is extendible to the airspace above the territorial sea and to the surface and subsoil of the seabed of the maritime belt.[63]

Relative to the limits of the territorial sea, Section 11, Article 3 delineates the normal base line for measurement of the breadth of the territorial sea as the low-water line along the coast as indicated on large-scale charts which have official acceptance by the coastal state.[64]

Article 4 provides that in localities where the coastline is deeply indented and has divisions, or if there is a border of islands along the coast and close to it, straight base lines connecting appropriate points may be utilized in drawing the base line from which the breadth of the territorial sea may be ascertained. Such base lines as are established may not appreciably deviate from the general direction of the coast, and the sea areas situated within such lines must be closely connected to the land surface to be subject to the regime of internal waters. It is further stipulated that base lines shall not be designated to and from low-tide altitudes, unless lighthouses or similar structures have been erected upon them and are regarded as constantly above sea level. When the method of straight base lines is applicable under provisory clauses of Paragraph 1, in the determination of special base lines, consideration may be directed to economic interests characteristic of the regional area, in relationship to apparent long usage. The system of straight base lines is not to be applied by a state if such action precludes free entry of the territorial sea of another state to the high seas. Moreover, the coastal state is required to indicate straight base lines on charts which have been duly publicized.[65]

Under provisions set forth in Article 5, waters on the landward side of the base line of the territorial sea constitute a portion of the internal waters of the state. However, in instances where the establishment of a straight base line under terms enunciated in Article 4 results in the enclosure of internal waters which previously had been regarded as a portion of the territorial sea or of the high sea, under provisions contained in Articles 14 to 23, there exists in these waters a right of innocent passage. The outermost limit of the territorial sea "is the line every point of which is at a distance from the nearest point of the base line equal to the breadth of the territorial sea."[66]

Although there were forty-four signatory states among the eighty-six participating states, the Convention on the Territorial Sea and the Contiguous Zone failed to achieve a definitive concept concerning the breadth of the territorial sea or a graphic concept of contiguous zones. The twenty-three substantive articles contained in the convention synthesized the law of the territorial sea without signifying its specific breadth. Section II of the convention is titled "Limits of the Territorial Sea," yet those limits are formulated in nebulous, inconclusive terms: "The outer limit of the territorial sea is the line every point of which is at a distance from the nearest point of the base line equal to the breadth of the territorial sea."[67]

The Geneva Conference failed to reach the agreement prepared by the International Law Commission in its final articles in 1956. The commission had reached the conclusion that "international law does not permit an extension of the territorial sea beyond twelve miles." However, the convention which was adopted in 1958 failed to suggest a maximum or minimum limitation of the territorial sea.[68]

In considering the contiguous zone, the International Law Commission encountered no principle opposing the establishment of a contiguous zone, twelve miles in breadth, in which a state might exercise protection of its customs laws, together with fiscal and sanitary interests. It was implied that the powers to be conferred upon the coastal state concerning this area should be confined to protection of the specific interests which were set forth and that sovereignty over the zone should not be included, nor would there be alteration of the zone as comprising a portion of the high seas.[69]

Concerning the contiguous zone, Article 24 provides:

1. In a zone of the high seas contiguous to its territorial sea, the coastal state may exercise the control necessary to:

a. Prevent infringement of its customs, fiscal, immigration or sanitary regulations within its territory or territorial sea.

b. Punish infringement of the above regulations committed within its territory or territorial sea.

2. The contiguous zone may not extend beyond twelve miles from the base line from which the breadth of the territorial sea is measured. . . .[70]

Thus the contiguous zone serves limited purposes and can only be interpreted as part of the high seas.

Although the 1958 Conference again failed to determine the breadth of the territorial sea, it did designate a twelve-mile breadth for the contiguous zone. This is regarded as an inadequate provision.[71] It is recognized that a state's area of control over contiguous high seas may require variance because of the purpose of the control and because of certain local world situations existing at given periods. States do exercise limited control over contiguous zones of high seas of undetermined widths adjoining their coasts.[72]

Indubitably, despite concerted efforts by eminent jurists who acted as governmental representatives of various states, the Geneva Conferences of 1958 and 1960 failed to agree upon a definitive limitation concerning the territorial sea. It must, therefore, be conceded that the law remains uncertain, although the three-mile limit is recognized by approximately two-thirds of the maritime states.[73]

Freedom of the Seas

By universal consent, the world community for several centuries regarded the high seas as open and free to all peoples. In previous centuries, beginning with the Roman empire and continuing until the Renaissance, certain empires had laid unequivocal claims to exclusive jurisdiction over great areas of the high seas.[74] But during the seventeenth and eighteenth centuries national pretensions to vast oceanic expanses were confronted by effective opposition and were eventually relinquished.[75] The doctrine of maritime sovereignty, the principle of the freedom of the open sea, gradually emerged in conformity with obvious interests of maritime nations, since there were conflicting claims to identical portions of the open sea. The freedom of the open sea was, therefore, recognized as beneficial to the general interests of all states, and especially to the freedom of relationships between nations.

Inevitably, a distinction becomes essential between claims to territorial waters and jurisdictional claims of control upon the high seas.[76] If there is "freedom of the high seas," then these seas cannot be under the sovereignty of any one particular state. The "high seas," according to Article 1 in the Convention on the High Seas, include "all parts of the sea that are not included in the territorial sea or in the internal waters of a state."[77]

Thus, the equitable extent or delimitation of the territorial sea is a topic of international significance. Freedom of the seas as a principle of international law prohibits partition or appropriation of the high seas. However, freedom of the seas is under challenge at present because of encroachments by certain coastal states. Large areas of the high seas are unilaterally claimed by national domination. These national efforts include enlargement of the area of inland waters by drawing lines from headline to headline and then from this base line (which may be in actuality many miles at sea), measuring the width of the nation's territorial waters. Other states extend the width of their territorial waters by unilateral decree. Methodologically, claims have been made for exclusive sovereignty over the waters above the continental shelf and above territorial waters. Certain exaggerated claims to territorial waters have extended to a breadth of two hundred miles as a seaward boundary.[78]

Right of Innocent Passage

Based upon numerous treaties and a process of gradualism, a doctrine of international customary law has emerged under which alien merchantmen have restricted right of innocent passage through the territorial seas of a coastal state.[79] The right of innocent passage through territorial waters does not, however, provide for access to national internal waters and ports. Thus the coastal state may exercise exclusive sovereignty and jurisdiction in these waters. As previously indicated, territorial sovereignty includes lakes, rivers, and areas of sea enclosed by various portions of the state's territory.

Within the territorial sea, the most significant limitation on the coastal state's plenary sovereignty is the servitude of innocent passage for vessels possessed by other states or nationals. It is the preponderant view that the right of innocent passage extends to foreign warships, especially in international straits, as well as to merchant ships. Except in international straits, it is conceded that coastal states may exercise temporary suspension of the right of innocent passage in specified areas of the territorial sea.[80]

The right of innocent passage afforded to foreign shipping in the territorial sea has not been extended to internal waters. This difference, however, would not modify the juridical status of this area of the sea for the purposes of this study, in that these waters are areas in which the coastal state may reserve for national purposes or for its nationals the right of both the use and the exploitation of existent oceanic resources.[81]

The dominant claims made by states over the territorial sea are often delineated in terms applicable to internal waters as affirmations of sovereignty over a portion of state territory. Particular claims concerning asserted sovereignty include the right to exclusive appropriation of resources within the area. The principal oppositional claim relative to access and navigation is ordinarily stated in terms of the concept of innocent passage.[82]

Breadth of the Territorial Sea

The divergence of views regarding the breadth of the territorial sea and the need for clarification and uniformity, having been recognized, comprehensive preparatory plans were made preceding the Convention on the Territorial Sea and the Contiguous Zone. The objective was to reach agreement on a convention applicable to territorial waters. The making of such plans required a period of years, in which various governments reached agreement on the fact that the subject of territorial waters was not only appropriate for consideration but urgently in need of codification.[83] In conjunction with efforts of the Committee of Experts and of the Preparatory Committee, the respective governments responded to numerous questionnaires and made comments concerning detailed schedules of data to serve as a predicate for discussions. All preliminary work was completed and printed months before the conference was held. Administrative processes of the entire conference and of the Commission on Territorial Waters were arranged to facilitate the consideration of these plans.

Despite the presence of well-formulated plans and well-informed delegates, however, the conference failed to clarify and reach agreement on one of the most significant subjects in international law—territorial waters.[84]

A multitude of conflicting claims were set forth by states in efforts to exercise national jurisdiction. Diversity of position was reflected in various governmental responses. Almost without exception, each of the participating states represented in the commission had a common interest both in navigational freedom of the high seas and in the retention of its authority over the littoral waters. Yet there existed critical variance of opinions based upon national geographic configurations.

Nevertheless, some constructive results did ultimately emerge. To a report adopted by the commission was affixed an annex which served as the basis of a draft on the fundamental status of the territorial sea. This draft, the fragile evidence of meager success, remained as an annex to a report which by the broadest interpretation might serve as foundation for a subsequent conference concerning codification of the law of territorial waters.[85]

Previously, two experiments in codification had been made: one was under the auspices of the League of Nations, the other under the aegis of the Pan-American Conferences. It will be recalled that one of the three pertinent topics on the agenda of the Conference for the Codification of International Law held under the patronage of the League in 1930 at The Hague was the "Regime of the Territorial Sea." Largely because of the divergence in views on the breadth to be ascribed to that area of the sea, the conference was unsuccessful in reaching definitive conclusions; yet its deliberations revealed the scope of the problems to be considered and achieved the formulation of basic concepts which were to be embodied subsequently in the international law of the sea.[86]

Still further efforts were begun after World War II when new international organizations undertook the monumental task of developing and codifying international law. This effort was stimulated by the fact that certain states issued declarations and enacted legislation following two proclamations of the President of the United States (1945) concerning the continental shelf and the conservation of fisheries.[87] At this crucial point, initiative was taken by the International Law Commission of the United Nations.

At its initial session held at Lake Success in 1949, the International Law Commission considered the "Regime of the High Sea" a topic deserving codification. Later in the year, the General Assembly recommended that such topics as the "Regime of the Territorial Sea" be included. Reports on the subjects by the special rapporteur, Professor François, were considered by the commission together with comprehensive observations made by governments. Various drafts were presented on two aspects of the "Regime of the High Seas," the "Continental Shelf" and "Fisheries."[88]

Action was deferred until all phases of the subject might be included in the deliberations. The commission's assignment was completed at its eighth session, and its work on the law of the sea was submitted to the General Assembly.[89]

At its eleventh session (1956), the General Assembly of the United Nations accepted the final report presented by the International Law Commission. In conformity with recommendations made by the commission, the decision was made to convene an international conference of plenipotentiaries to examine the law of the sea and to incorporate the results of its deliberations in one or more international conventions. Thereafter, the United Nations Conference on the Law of the Sea convened in Geneva from February 24 to April 29, 1958.[90]

Eighty-five states sent representatives to the conference; specialized agencies of the United Nations, as well as intergovernmental bodies, sent observers. The General Assembly resolution adopting the report of the International Law Commission was accepted as the basic document for consideration.[91]

As has been said earlier, agreement failed on two significant questions: the breadth of the territorial sea and certain fishery claims.[92]

Historically, by the late Middle Ages the accepted concept of the territorial sea was that of a possessory right by the coastal states. Since then, however, there has been no clearly defined concept. Indubitably, the territorial sea has been associated by the majority of states with the concept of exclusiveness accruing to the benefit of the littoral state, with the exception of certain limitations acknowledged as essential for the protection of interests and rights of other states. Questions have been posed as to whether the concept of exclusiveness is derived from property right, sovereignty, dominion, or imperium, or upon a theory of jurisdiction. Lack of uniformity is evidenced by the various ways in which states have claimed rights in this area of the sea in their respective constitutions, in legislative enactments, or through variance of opinion expressed in multilateral treaties.[93]

Fundamentally, the rights of the littoral state in its territorial sea are deemed analogous to those which are recognized in its territorial land areas, over which international law permits the coastal state to exercise plenary authority. The origin of the legal concepts concerning rights of the littoral states is unimportant in comparison with the dominant concept of "exclusiveness" which characterize the rights. The premise of rights was considered by the Second Committee of the Codification Conference of The Hague in its inclusion of the term "sovereignty" in Article 1 of its draft.[94] In comments on this article in its report, the subcommittee observed that

the idea which it has been sought to express by stating that the belt of territorial sea forms part of the territory of the state is that the power exercised by the state over this belt is in its nature no different from the power which the state exercises over its domain on land. This is also the reason why the term "sovereignty" has been retained, a term which better than any other describes the juridical nature of this power.[95]

The juridical status of the territorial sea was defined by the International Law Commission in Article 1 of its draft, stating in substance that the *sovereignty* of a state extends to a belt of sea which is adjacent to its coasts. In both drafts this sovereign right of a coastal state is based upon recognition of certain limitations which constitute a servitude superimposed by international law. The legal status of the territorial sea was set forth in the convention on the issue by the Geneva Conference.[96]

A number of different questions have been raised concerning the breadth of the territorial sea. One question is whether or not the width of the territorial sea has been established by international law. As is well known, there has been a lack of uniformity in practice concerning the breadth of the territorial sea. Also, it has been asserted that no rule of international law is unequivocally established on the subject. Other inquiries are related to the question of whether the breadth of the territorial sea may properly be determined by international law or whether the issues are within the sovereignty or exclusive competence of the littoral state. Is the question capable of solution by this body of law, and is a coastal state, in regard to the breadth of the territorial sea, subject to regulatory measures imposed by international law?[97]

It is recognized that within concepts concerning the territorial sea there exists a repository of judicial rights, as well as obligations, for the coastal state. A question may be interposed concerning the possible inadequacy of the traditional minimum breadth of three miles and the establishment of criteria for the coastal state to extend its territorial sea beyond that limit. Historically, the criterion was effective exercise of power; however, currently there is emphasis upon geographical and geological considerations, together with biological factors of the marine zone contiguous to the territory of the state, the economic and social aspects, and interests of given nationals. A fixed jurisdictional limit of the territorial seas presents difficulties in application to all maritime states, irrespective of geographical or geological variance, particular needs of states, and specific regional characteristics.[98]

The inadequacy of the three-mile limit has been proclaimed by certain states. May the coastal state extend its territorial sea to an unreasonable limit? Should a maximum limit be established irrespective of the criteria supporting the specific breadth? May the littoral state claim one limit to its territorial sea for certain purposes and still other limits for other purposes? May the territorial sea be regarded as "indivisible" or in terms of "plurality"? Moreover, the method utilized for the delimitation of the territorial sea may affect the regime controlling the use and exploitation of the resources of the sea.[99]

It is conceded that while there is no complete uniformity in principle or practice regarding the breadth of the territorial sea, yet it is admitted that for many years there has been consensus as to the breadth of this area. Traditional international law recognized the marine league, that is, the limit of three nautical miles.[100]

Origin and Development of the Three-Mile Limit

As a juridical concept, there is an indissoluble interrelationship between the territorial sea and the principle of the freedom of the high seas. To recapitulate briefly, the Roman jurists regarded the sea as *Mare Liberum*. Commercial development in the Middle Ages contributed to the creation of claims by maritime nations for exclusive control over areas of the open sea contiguous to their respective territories. Exaggerated claims reached maximum heights toward the close of the fifteenth century when Spain made claims of exclusive navigational rights, indistinguishable from ownership, in the Pacific Ocean, the Gulf of Mexico, and the Western Atlantic Ocean; Portugal, in like manner, made equivalent claims in the Atlantic south of Morocco and the entire Indian Ocean. Great Britain initiated claims to the Narrow Seas and the North Sea. Legal concepts in these claims were negligible, since assertions by various nations were recognized in proportion to prowess in defense measures. This practice was according to the doctrine of *Mare Clausum*. (Grotius made one of the first zealous attacks on these extensive claims to sovereignty.)[101]

However, a reversion to the Roman doctrine of freedom of the seas in the seventeenth century achieved acceptance. Thereafter, general navigational rights in the open seas motivated reluctance on the part of nations to acquiesce in complete freedom of navigation touching the immediate shorelines of given nations.[102] Imperative issues involved the interests of national security and self-defense, together with protection of neutral shipping in periods of war. These vital issues led to the necessity for a maritime nation to exercise jurisdiction over the waters adjacent to its coast to an undetermined distance from shore. Early jurists and publicists were unable to agree with exactitude on a specific distance because of lack of perception of a definite guiding principle. There were assertions that the distance of the territorial sea should extend for one hundred miles from the coast; other suggestions were made that the distance should extend to sailing time for a given number of days or to the distance of sight.[103] Ultimately, the "cannon-shot" rule was introduced—that is, the distance from shore that a nation possessed capability of defense. The distance to which a cannon could be effectively discharged was the determining factor in measurement for ascertaining jurisdictional limits. By the mid-eighteenth century, this definition of the maritime boundary of a state was gaining acceptance. The range of cannon during the eighteenth century was approximately three nautical miles or a marine league; this distance was, therefore, accepted as the limit to which a coastal nation could exercise territorial jurisdiction.[104]

Another view of the origin of the three-mile limit is that the concept originated in Denmark-Norway and was prevalent there from the late sixteenth to the early nineteenth century.[105]

The practice of exercising jurisdiction within adjoining maritime areas of a standard width came into customary use in Denmark without consideration of the cannon-shot rule. Jurisdictional claims attributed to Danish custom were based on a *dominium maris* or on still earlier practices which set forth claims to waters situated within sight of land. The earliest regulatory measures concerning jurisdiction within a continuous belt of fixed measurement were the result of pressures exerted by foreign traders and fishermen. Danish sea power was inadequate to enforce claims to a *dominium maris* or to wide belts of contiguous waters against powerful maritime nations such as Holland, France, and Britain. Hence the acceptance by Denmark of a narrower jurisdictional limit. Disputes with other powers contributed to Danish retreats in 1602. In armed conflicts, Danish neutrality was conceded by maritime nations by recognition of a continuous neutral belt, rather than zones protected by cannon-shot. A proposal was made by France that the width of the continuous belt be modified to three miles, the possible range of cannon. Whatever the reason, Denmark (including Norway) introduced the league as the limit for fishery purposes in 1743. Thus the three-mile limit of territorial jurisdiction within a continuous belt of standard width is a precept attributable to Danish-Norwegian practice (1812), rather than to the cannon-shot dictum.[106]

During the nineteenth century, the three-mile limit for the territorial sea remained virtually unchallenged in practice. Its acceptance was recognized by formal documents and by eminent statesmen. Few countries formally opposed the three-mile limit during this period.[107]

The dictum prevails that the coastal state has sovereignty over its territorial sea. Moreover, monopolistic practices by coastal states concerning resources contained within their territorial seas have had general acceptance. (Exclusive fishing rights within the territorial sea are subject to modification by the repudiation of the privilege by the coastal state or by process of governmental concurrence.)

Certain authors contended that the three-mile limit was not within the purview of assertions made by Grotius in 1609, in which he successfully supported the doctrine of *res communis*, that the high seas were the common property of all nations. The significance of this doctrine was that no state might unilaterally appropriate any portion of the high seas without the general consent of all states.[108] Two centuries later claims were first made containing the modern concept of a territorial sea. However, by that time the principle of the freedom of the seas had crystallized, and the concept that the high seas are *res communis* was established in international law.[109]

Certain authors and statesmen have erroneously connected the cannon-shot three-mile limit and the modern territorial sea. But the cannon-shot rule was important because it afforded a foundation for assertions, in given limited situations, of the right of free navigation.

Historically, in 1702 the Dutch publicist Cornelius van Bynkershoek stated the rule in terminology which was accepted as authoritative, namely, that a nation might exercise sovereignty over waters which were within cannon range of its shoreline, that three miles constituted the range of cannon. Therefore, certain authors regarded Bynkershoek as the originator of the three-mile limit. However, more recent scholarship has disclosed that the cannon-shot rule was practiced by states prior to Bynkershoek's pronouncements and that the range of cannon in his era and for a century later was considerably less than three miles. The conclusion was that the seventeenth- and eighteenth-century practice of the cannon-shot rule was unrelated to the modern conception of territorial jurisdiction or sovereignty.[110] It has been observed that Bynkershoek failed to mention the distance of three miles.[111]

For purposes of neutrality, the cannon-shot rule sanctioned the right of protective jurisdiction within areas extending seaward no more than one or two miles from cannon located on shore. Obviously, the rule did not conform to a uniform breadth within the zone or to a three-mile distance. The rule did not permit the exercise by the littoral state of territorial jurisdiction over any portion of the high sea.[112]

A new concept emerged during the early nineteenth century: the cannon-shot dictum, reiterated by various powers to support the principal of freedom of the seas, was superseded by the modern theory of the three-mile limit for national jurisdiction in the territorial sea. The one-league limit was adopted into state practice. The concept recognized that the littoral state may exercise "full and absolute territorial jurisdiction" within a margin of sea one maritime league in breadth along its coast.[113] This doctrine was applied by England to fishing and other relevant matters, together with neutrality. The United States and other coastal states accepted an English league or three miles as the proper limit of territorial jurisdiction. Cannon-range became the equivalent of three miles.[114] Conversely, the Swedish, Danish, and Norwegian neutrality zones based upon a breadth of one German league, the equivalent of four nautical miles, became the foundation for their claims regarding their territorial seas. Denmark, however, now adheres to the territorial limit of an English league or three nautical miles. The extension by the coastal states of their seaward boundaries to a three-mile distance constituted an appropriation of the *res communis* of the high seas, and was invalid until approved by the general consent of nations.[115] By the early part of the twentieth century, substantially all states had at least tacitly agreed to acceptance of the three-mile limit or one league. Thereafter that limit was established as a customary rule of international law by the community of nations.[116] The more specific maritime boundary was accepted by the major powers, including Great Britain and the United States, as indicating the extreme boundary of territorial sovereignty, while certain other maritime states claimed wider areas of the territorial sea.

Although it is conceded that the sovereignty of the coastal state does not extend beyond the territorial sea into the area designated as the high seas, such a coastal state may exercise reasonable control over foreign ships in zones contiguous to its territorial sea. This extension of control is a protective measure to prevent violations within its territorial boundaries of its security and its customs, immigration, fiscal, or sanitary regulations. It is widely recognized that a coastal state may exercise exclusive jurisdiction and control, tantamount to sovereignty, over the natural resources of the sea floor adjacent to its land territory, together with the subsoil to the greatest depth at which the exploitation of such resources is feasible (the "continental shelf" doctrine). The coastal state may, moreover, not only pursue but seize a foreign vessel on the high seas for the violation of its laws, provided the pursuit was started within its territorial sea or contiguous zone and that the pursuit has been continuous ("hot pursuit").[117]

The Six-Mile Limit

Various nations have exercised control and jurisdiction on the high seas adjacent to territorial waters.[118] The fundamental question concerning the law of the sea is inextricably associated with the breadth of the belt to which the territorial sovereignty of the littoral state extends. As has been indicated, nineteenth-century practice made a distinction between the plenary character of a littoral state's jurisdiction in its territorial waters and its right of assertion to limited jurisdiction on the high seas. Certain coastal states declared specific rights on the high seas.[119] The most salient claims in coastal state assertions of jurisdiction in its territorial sea were in regard to anti-smuggling laws and regulations affecting dutiable articles. Later in the century, eminent English and American jurists conceded distinctions between the general or "territorial" jurisdiction of a littoral state on its land and in a limited narrow zone adjacent to its coast and the wider, special jurisdiction over which the state purported to enforce its fiscal laws. In a celebrated dictum,[120] Mr. Chief Justice Marshall recognized the distinction between a state's absolute and exclusive jurisdiction within its territory and its limited power to utilize reasonable means to capture ships on the sea beyond that territorial boundary on grounds of suspicion of illicit or contraband trade.

Following the inconclusive deliberations of the 1958 and 1960 conferences, and the failure to define the breadth of the territorial sea, unilateral declarations have purported to submit large areas of the high seas to the exclusive jurisdiction of the coastal states. These practices must be generally considered as incompatible with accepted principles of international law.[121] At the time of the Hague Conference in 1930, approximately eight of the thirty-eight coastal states claimed more than one league of territorial waters, but no plenary assertions of jurisdiction beyond three miles by these states were apparently exercised in the first thirty years of the twentieth century.[122] Related questions that have been raised are concerned with ascertaining the nature of the sovereign rights that the littoral state can exercise over its territorial waters and determining whether questions pertaining to these rights relate also to the rights and obligations of states on the high seas.[123] If the limit is extended seaward, the need is lessened for the exercise of exceptional powers on the high seas, and the need is increased for exceptions to the powers of the littoral state over foreign ships utilizing its territorial waters.[124]

The crucial nature of the question, together with the substantial economic and political elements involved, have made the problem one of the most controversial issues in contemporary international law. Though for more than a century and a half great maritime nations adhered to the three-mile rule, the rule was never universally accepted. Exceptions occurred in the practice of the Scandinavian countries in adopting a four-mile limit and in the adoption by certain Mediterranean countries of the six-mile rule. Moreover, Czarist Russia adopted a twelve-mile limit for certain purposes. Despite the lack of consistency and uniformity, early in the twentieth century there existed authority for the view that due to the practice of the great maritime nations there had been established a customary rule of international law. In conformity with this customary law, all littoral states were entitled to a territorial sea of three miles, and, therefore, no state could claim a greater breadth of territorial sea in the absence of a definite historic title.[125]

The undeviating adherence to the three-mile rule by major maritime countries prevented the Hague Conference in 1930 from reaching an acceptable solution Since this failure to reach a uniform limit of the territorial sea, there has been a persistent and continuing tendency in state practice to extend the limits. At the Geneva Conference in 1958, only approximately twenty coastal states out of seventy-three were adherents of the three-mile rule.

Specific claims of a six-mile zone for the breadth of the territorial sea have been made by certain states including Ceylon, Greece, Haiti, India, Iran, Israel, Italy, Libya, Yugoslavia, and Spain. (In 1906, Spain enacted legislation prohibiting fishing by all foreigners within six miles of its shores).[126] It has been observed that since a modern territorial sea constitutes a claim of extension of a state's plenary jurisdiction or seaward offshore boundary beyond its coastline, and since *ad hoc* claims to a territorial sea for limited purposes such as customs rights, sanitary regulations, and security are doubtful, such claims should not be cited as evidence of a claim to more than one league. It has been stated further that virtually all states which have only such claims have been included in the list of states claiming more than one league unless the state concerned has clearly indicated that its claim is a limited one or that its claim does not include plenary jurisdiction beyond one league. Moreover, the *ad hoc* claims lack uniformity and, therefore, given claims may not constitute a claim to plenary jurisdiction.[127]

The Twelve-Mile Limit

In the autumn of 1958 attention was focused on a controversy between British and Icelandic vessels because of the unilateral effort of Iceland to extend its seaward boundary to twelve miles, for exclusive fishing rights, and on the refusal of the United States to accept Communist China's territorial extension seaward beyond the customary three-mile limit.[128]

The doctrine of *res communis* is in jeopardy when unilateral action is invoked to alter the existing rule limiting the breadth of the territorial sea. In the Icelandic claim, the consequences were less significant, in that the claim affected only a limited right to regulate fishing in an area beyond Iceland's territorial sea. The claim of Communist China, on the other hand, should be analyzed in the context of the genesis of the modern concept of the territorial sea and its inseparable connection with the *res communis* doctrine that the high seas are the common property of all nations.[129] The great significance of the fact that the high seas are *res communis* is that no portion of the high seas may be unilaterally appropriated without the general consent of other states.

In actions violating the *res communis* doctrine, the breadth of the territorial sea has been unilaterally extended to the twelve-mile limit by certain states including Bulgaria, Colombia, Ethiopia, Guatemala, Indonesia, Rumania, Saudi Arabia, Union of Soviet Socialist Republics, United Arab Republic, Venezuela, and El Salvador.[130] In 1952, by presidential proclamation, Korea asserted national sovereignty over the seas adjacent to its coast varying between twenty and two hundred miles in breadth for purposes of conservation, protection, and utilization of the resources of the sea.[131]

The 1958 conference reached agreement upon significant issues relative to the breadth of the territorial sea. New encroachments upon the freedom of the seas required demonstrable justification, and then only a grant of limited jurisdiction was tolerated. Extension of the seaward boundary was prohibited. Freedom of the seas is under challenge at present, however, because of encroachments by small coastal states. Large areas of the high seas are unilaterally claimed by national dominion, by enlargement of the area of inland waters. Lines are drawn from headland to headland, and from this base line, which may be many miles at sea, the territorial waters of the states are measured. Other states by unilateral decree extend the width of their territorial waters.[132]

Zones up to Two Hundred Miles

In the Declaration on Maritime Zones, proclaimed in 1952, Chile, Ecuador, and Peru issued a decree of exclusive sovereignty and jurisdiction over oceanic waters contiguous to their respective coasts to a minimum distance seaward of two hundred miles.[133] These three nations signed the Declaration of Santiago on August 18, 1952, claiming "exclusive jurisdiction and sovereignty" over waters adjacent to their given coastlines extending to a minimum distance of two hundred nautical miles seaward, together with exclusive sovereignty over the soilbed and subsoil in this maritime zone. Protests from the United States set forth objections to these claims on the basis that under international law there exists an obligation for international recognition of claims to territorial waters in excess of the three-mile zone.

Certain Central and South American states, including El Salvador, Honduras, and Argentina, have instituted claims to large areas of the high seas as territorial waters.[134]

Thus, the unilateral claims of certain nations extending the breadth of the terriorial sea constitute a process of encroachment upon the internationally sanctioned doctrine of *res communis* which endangers the future status of the freedom of the seas.

State Sovereignty

The word "sovereignty" lacks precise definition in the literature of international law, for generations of jurists and political scientists have failed to define it with exactitude. The term implies a relationship of superiority and subordination. Debates have ensued for two centuries to determine whether the relationship is absolute or relative in degree.[135]

State territory is definable as that area of the surface of the globe which is under the authority of the autonomous state and which is governed by its laws. The territory of a state is under the protection of the sovereign power. Moreover, state territory may be designated as the territorial property of a state pertaining to public law in contra-distinction to private property. The territory of a state is not the possession of the government, or of the citizenry of a state; the country is under the dominion of the *imperium* of a state. The significance of state territory is the truism that it is the geographical area within which the state exercises dominant authority.[136]

As to the juridical character of the territorial sea, it may be asked whether territorial waters are juridically assimilable with land areas to the point that the coastal state has jurisdiction over such waters and moreover possesses them inclusively within its national boundary.[137] The question no longer remains an academic inquiry but has advanced to international significance since the conveyance by certain states of property rights in the territorial sea for the exploitation of mineral resources.

Theoretical views on the subject have included the position that the territorial waters constitute an appendage to the land segment and may, therefore, be construed as an area within the national boundary. The territorial sea has been regarded by certain theorists as an aggregation of jurisdictional rights. Following this opinion, the coastal state is invested by international law with a limited number of capacities, in regard to piscatorial rights, revenue, police, and neutrality. The high sea, however, remains *res communis* and is therefore beyond the national boundary. Geographically, the sea is an entity, incapable of partition. For reasons of security measures a state may exercise rights upon the sea. These rights are categorized by reference to the high seas and the territorial sea, but permissive rights enjoyed by the coastal state do not include possessive rights in the sea.[138]

Another view regards the territorial sea as subject to sovereignty but remaining outside the area of national territorial boundary. This view endorses the opinion that for general purposes the coastal state's jurisdiction is indeterminate or indistinguishable from sovereignty, except for the recognized existence of a right of innocent passage through territorial waters. This servitude precludes absolute dominion over the area. Therefore, the coastal state has limited jurisdictional rights rather than plenary authority. There is no power of disposition of any portion of the territorial sea or of its bed. The coastal state has certain recognized rights of necessity, which detract from the status of the sea as *res communis*. The suggestion that the territorial sea includes servitudes necessarily precludes sovereignty from the territorial sea.[139]

Conservation rights are emphasized in other theories regarding the territorial sea. These opinions accord to the coastal state only such specified measurements as are essential for defense of its population and material affluence. Strictly, the territorial sea cannot be assimilated to land territory but serves as an assurance for relevant commercial activities and public revenues to the littoral citizenry.[140]

The territorial sea, for other theorists, constitutes a portion of the public domain and is the subject of *imperium* and *dominium* except for the fact that ships of all nations have a right of passage over it.[141] In regard to the juridical nature of the territorial sea in international law, there emerges the problem of ascertaining whether the sea is geographically within the national boundary, or constitutes an appendage to the national domain. International law can only define the maximum jurisdiction over the territorial sea. The phraseology employed in proclamations, enactments, and other documents relative to appropriation of or national assertions of claims over submarine areas fails to clarify the question of whether such rights pertain to sovereignty or constitute merely jurisdictional rights and control.[142]

During the past thirty years there has been an accelerated tendency to refer to "sovereignty" over the territorial sea in various international transactions. The majority of the states presenting opinions to the Preparatory Committee for the Conference for the Codification of International Law in 1927 and those sending observations concerning the drafts of the International Law Commission consented to the employment of the term "sovereignty" as applied to territorial waters. Article I of the Final Act on the Territorial Sea at Geneva provided that the sovereignty of a state extends, beyond its land territory and internal waters, to a margin of sea contiguous to its coast, designated as the territorial sea.

Since the specific breadth of the territorial sea is undetermined in international law, the question of sovereignty or jurisdictional rights is surrounded by interpretive ambiguity and lacks cogent conclusions.

Political Interests

It has been observed that the urgent necessity for expansive scientific research in the ocean, entailing access to all areas of the ocean both in contiguous waters and at remote distances from land, represents a poignant contrast in recent trends in the law of the sea. The dominant trend, during the past decade, is an incisive national expansionism of "exclusive state authority over the ocean."[144] For centuries negligible attention was directed to the extent of oceanic boundaries except during periods of tension or warfare. Since World War II, the significance of the resources of the sea has engaged the attention of individuals and nations. There has been an urgent realization that within the world ocean or "inner space" there exists a vast reservoir of deposits of mineral resources, nonliving resources, as well as living resources, awaiting technological feasibility for exploitation and utilization by the world community.[145] There has been an emphasis upon the food potentiality[146] within this domain, especially among emerging nations, and upon the importance of mineral wealth as a means of military defense and national security. In view of the incalculable potentialities of the ocean's resources, many states have made unilateral revisions of customary boundaries and established more extensive ones. Within the past decade, certain states have incorporated within state territory areas of the contiguous ocean and sea-floor, even when the unilateral declarations involved serious political implications.[147]

Politically, a new epoch has been initiated through technological and scientific advancement in various aspects of oceanography. A new era in the uses of the sea has evolved with the availability of different construction materials, new methods of propulsion, and new instruments for purposes of observation and for navigation, as well as for international communications. A multiplicity of devices provide essential instrumentalities for the exploration of ocean depths and for the exploitation of animate and inanimate resources of the sea.[148] Within the immediate future legitimate political advantage, economic advancement, and the attainment of basic knowledge of the sea and its hostile environment will be within reach. Engineering successes illustrate our present ability to make progress in oceanography.

However, technical progress alone is an inadequate basis for the formulation of political policies affecting development and utilization of marine resources.[149] Uses of the sea, the economic and social advantages of projected oceanic activities, must be examined from two points of view: that of the ever broadening opportunities created by scientific discovery, and that of the kaleidoscopic potential of the sea to meet significant challenges which confront the nations and the collective populace of all nations. International collaboration is essential in many areas. Limits of sovereignty demand clarification and agreement among political powers. Methods need to be devised for the mobilization of industrial entrepreneurships, financial structures, and governments. Responding to the innumerable political complexities, challenging proposals for solutions are being presented by individuals, certain statesmen, and representatives of nations.[150]

Economic Interests

The worldwide phenomenon of legal, political, and security interest in oceanic areas is translated into the realm of economic interests of the world community. At the present time the United States, as one of the nations of this community, has developed unprecedented productive economic and industrial complexes. This gargantuan complex is dependent upon $32 billion worth of exports and imports conveyed annually through waterborne commerce. At present, an estimated half of the free world's mineral production is diverted to the requirements of the American industrial complex.[151] In certain critical items, such as tin, manganese and chromite, there is consumption within domestic areas of the United States in excess of one-fifth of the world's total production. Since the national economy is dependent upon the importation of these items, it is essential that navigational freedoms be maintained without impediment. Air commercial cargoes (export and import) are minimal in comparison with sea cargoes. In one respect, therefore, the United States is highly dependent on freedom of the seas.

Conversely, the United States is extensively engaged in exploratory efforts in developmental aspects of oceanographic activities and in the recovery of ocean resources in local waters and in many other areas of the world ocean. United States private industries are investing substantial sums in exploration and drilling projects for petroleum, in capital and labor in fisheries, in coastal development, in marine transportation, and in other uses of the ocean.[152] There has been an accrual of vast revenues resulting from these endeavors. During the past twenty years, the United States Treasury has collected as bonuses, rentals, and royalties on offshore oil and gas leases sums exceeding

$3 billion. Royalties alone in 1968 approximated $200 million. Coastal states also collected substantial sums. The international decade of ocean exploration will initiate investigations concerning the rationalization, protection, and extension of economic opportunities for capital investments off continental coasts in many areas of the world.[153]

The Marine Resources and Development Act of 1966[154] set forth national objectives in the marine environment; the term "marine environment" included:

(a) the oceans, (b) the Continental Shelf of the United States, (c) the Great Lakes, (d) sea-bed and subsoil of the submarine areas adjacent to the coasts of the United States to the depth of two hundred meters, or beyond that limit, to where the depths of the superjacent waters admit of the natural resources of such areas, (e) the sea-bed and subsoil of similar submarine areas adjacent to the coasts of islands which comprise United States' territory, and (f) the resources thereof.[155]

This act, in conjunction with the Outer Continental Shelf Act, undergirds the potential jurisdiction beyond the three-mile and three-league limits to a depth of two hundred meters, or beyond, if competency exists or can be achieved, for exploitation of natural resources in deeper areas. The area of the oceans from shore to two-hundred-meter contour alone includes approximately one million square miles.[156]

Thus the United States, like other coastal nations, is confronted with the dilemma of unilateral expansionism seaward and the ancient legal order of free seas.

It may be anticipated that population and political demands will ultimately induce all industrialized nations to recover many minerals from the sea. Engineering projections indicate that the mining of many materials from the marine environment would be economically feasible. It is predicted that within a generation the sea will provide a major source of metals.[157]

Within the ocean, through natural processes, the separation and concentration of the elements which enter sea water forms minerals in high concentrations on the sea floor. Ultimately technological progress and reduction in power costs will make feasible the utilization of common rocks for the production of ample minerals for all purposes. The sediments of the ocean will probably be used initially, since pelagic sediments contain approximately ten times the amount of industrially essential metals contained in the igneous rocks on land.

They are widely distributed in the proximity of most markets and are available to all nations. These materials are unconsolidated and are located in a water atmosphere which makes feasible the use of automated hydraulic system for exploitation. Present indications are that in future years mineral resources may be recovered to greater economic advantage from the sea than from land sources.[158]

Manganese nodules are among the most interesting of mineral deposits in the sea. Indications have been obtained through calculations and laboratory tests that existing industrial equipment and processes may be successfully adapted to mining the manganese nodules. If various metals contained in the nodules may be economically mined, or if only 10 percent of the nodule deposits which occur on the surface of the sediments of the Pacific Ocean alone are feasibly recoverable, it is estimated that sufficient quantities of metal supplies exist in the sea-floor deposits to constitute an ever increasing reserve for thousands of years at present calculations of consumption.[159] Through natural processes mineral deposits would increase with greater rapidity than the speed of extraction by mining recovery systems.

The composition of the nodules varies substantially at various locations on the ocean floor. These nodules, which are irregularly spherical in shape, are ordinarily found on the surface of the ocean floor at depths varying from 4,500 to 19,000 feet. Concentration and distribution of the nodules differ in various geographical areas. Maximum known metal content of various nodules has been computed as 57.1 percent manganese, 39.5 percent iron, 2.9 percent copper, 2.4 percent nickel, 2.1 percent cobalt, etc. Tentative tonnage computations for Pacific Ocean nodules, based on inadequate knowledge of the extent of deposits, vary from 9 to 170 trillion tons.[160] Ten thousand tons per day would be necessary for economical mining.

Another factor is the mineral content of the waters of the high seas, which, irrespective of sea floor sedimentation, amalgamation, granules, or deposits, constitutes a major source of wealth.[161]

Ocean industries form a superstructure of heterogeneous activities with diverse operational requisites, investment deviations, competitive practices, and relationships with government in regard to general marine enterprises, and with special requirements for given industries and components.[162]

The dockside evaluation of resources from the shelf and waters adjacent to the United States exploited by U.S. entrepreneurs was quoted in 1967 as an estimated $2 billion annually.[163]

Undersea operations, whether fixed or mobile, are dependent upon supplies. No single type of power source is presently available, nor is any apt to be feasible, for all power requirements, levels of endurance, and ambient pressure needs of undersea activities. A combination of power sources with various characteristics will be required. As marine industries penetrate into greater oceanic depths and extend farther from shore, self-sustaining power supplies will be essential. This requirement will be supplied by a single system or a combination of several: cables, batteries, fuel cells, isotopes, thermal conversion systems, and other types.[164]

In the consideration of mineral resources of the sea, a distinction should be made between minerals present in sea water and minerals which lie on or under the seabed. Commercially profitable items contained in sea water are ordinary salt, magnesium metal, and bromine. Also within this classification is fresh water.[165] These items, while they are of commercial significance, present no problem associated with international law, since recovery procedures are executed at shore installations within the jurisdictional sovereignty of a coastal state. Minerals of present commercial significance existing on or beneath the seabed are petroleum, natural gas, and sulfur; sand, gravel, and oyster shells; and tin, diamonds, and phosphate rock. These mineral resources are usually present near shore or on the continental shelves and are subject to existing legal regimes.[166]

Since economic concern with mineral resources of the marine environment have aroused worldwide interest in the ocean and its resources, it becomes essential to consider many questions, among them the classification of mineral sources, and their geographical location; the value of such resources in relationship to available minerals on land areas; and ownership of the oceanic mineral resources. Answers to these questions involve complexities in science, technology, economics, government, and law.[167]

The resources of the ocean may be considered in three major categories: chemical—materials dissolved in the water; biological—living resources of plant and animal life in the water; and geological—minerals that occur on or beneath the ocean floor. From the standpoint of resource value, the continental shelf is the greatest potential source of economic return. All of the chemical resources, all of the geological resources, and approximately 90 percent of the biological resources have been derived from the shelf. Greater increases in the productivity of the shelf may be predicted with technological developments, especially in chemical and geological resources. Attributable to this potential increase in recoverable minerals, and to accelerated market demands for such resources, is the fact that the shelf areas are the locale of increasing national claims and counterclaims regarding ownership and jurisdictional rights to levy taxes as well as rights of exploitation. The most strident national claims are made concerning geological resources, which are regarded as attached to the sea floor. Great claims are also made for the biological resources, most of which have restricted movement, because of the fact that their annual productive patterns are greater than the combined productions of geological and chemical resources, and because of world demands for food. Chemical resources, although of economic value, are in secondary demand because they are dissolved in water and move freely with the water.[168]

The list of recoverable marine resources consists of three major groups: authigenic, detrital, and organic. The authigenic minerals, phosphorite and manganese, are formed by chemical precipitation from sea water. Detrital minerals are transported to the ocean largely by streams or sea-cliff erosion and deposited as widely distributed layers on the sea floor. The detrital minerals are sand, gravel, titanium, zircon, tin, diamonds, monazite, iron, and gold. The term "detrital minerals" includes all minerals derived from erosion of rocks.[169] Organic minerals are oil, gas, and sulfur.

Certain proponents of sea-floor mining have prepared lists of minerals that have been recovered from the sea floor primarily by general scientific expeditions. However, some authorities contend that only a limited number of the minerals may be recovered at costs comparable to the costs of land production of similar quality.[170]

There have been proposals for new law concerning exploitation of recoverable resources from the marine environment. This law would be affected by consensus regarding the width of the territorial sea, the area in which the coastal state has sovereignty, inclusive of sovereign rights to exploitation of minerals. At present, clarification of that law is not of significant importance as far as mineral resources are concerned, since the continental shelf begins at the point where the territorial sea terminates, and under present conceptions and descriptions all coastal states, irrespective of geographical variation, have a continental shelf. Certain revisions in the definition of the shelf might, however, seriously affect ownership of mineral resources in connection with the width of the territorial sea.[171]

The need for exploration and exploitation of marine mineral resources arises in part from the fact that exploration of the landmasses is now substantially reduced, with the exception of central Australia, Greenland, portions of the Arctic and Antarctic, and probably areas of northern Siberia. In the exploration phase are included certain essential inquiries to ascertain what resources are actually available and economically exploitable. Exploitation of landmass resources continues at accelerated rates in mineral and petroleum products.[172] Known available landmass resources are accessible and their exploitation is technically feasible if the demands are of sufficient magnitude to warrant the capital investment for exploitation of a given area. Economic problems and demand are determining factors in the exploitation of oceanic resources. Ultimately such resources will be available. Meanwhile, the time element and costs of production are significant in making ocean-located resources accessible in view of equity capital requirement for the economic venture. Another essential consideration in the development of oceanic resources is the establishment of international means for the determination and recognition of ocean-floor claims and titles possessing the reliability of title acknowledged on land-based rights.[173] Improved navigational facilities will be essential to the establishment of accurate systems of claims and titles. Satellite navigation makes possible not only basic research but also surveying and drilling operations. Communications systems, including underwater telephone and television, satellite-scanning of vast ocean areas, and voice communications over the entire world, contribute immeasurably to oceanic endeavors.[174]

Overclouding advantageous aspects of economic interests, there are certain constraints on oceanic activities in marine resources. There is a lack of adequate underwater communications, due to the fact that electromagnetic energy cannot be transmitted through water. Above the waters, a competent engineer trained in radar may transmit and receive messages at 186,000 miles a second; but under water, with acoustics for communication, the speed is diminished to 4,920 feet per second. This handicap in speed, in conjunction with interference of temperature gradients, salinity, and additional biological elements, contributes to the problem of underwater communications.[175]

Lack of visibility and critical attenuation of the strongest light sources constitute a major hazard in oceanic depths and restrict operations in such depths to artificial light.

The physiology of underwater living represents another deterrent to development of undersea resources. Certain progress has been made in work ability at depths of approximately 650 feet. However, average depth of open seas is measured at 13,000 feet.

Labor laws and workmen's compensation laws enacted for the protection of workers will be inadequate for deep opaque oceanic waters; a new scale of values will be essential to establish the extent to which exposure to undersea living conditions will affect the protection of health and life expectancy.

Still another need is the establishment of legal rights concerning claims, titles, and locations. This difficulty may well preclude the acquisition of equity capital for entrepreneurial activities in given situations.[176]

Substantial basic knowledge exists concerning marine economic interest, together with engineering technology, for successful exploitation of certain mineral resources. However, there are also technical and applied engineering obstacles of considerable magnitude. Competent authority assures us that current technological and engineering strictures will be gradually diminished and eliminated. Industry and public demand will determine the utilization of oceanic resources when the demand is intensified and such resources are considered to be economically rational.[177]

Ocean Mining

Contemporary preoccupation with economic interests concerning utilization of marine mineral resources had its inception in remote periods of antiquity. Although the first claims made to certain resources, now known as the seabed of the continental shelf, were made centuries ago, the exact time is unknown. It may be inferred that the first claims occurred as early as the sixth century B.C.[178]

In a much-cited article, "Whose Is the Bed of the Sea?" Sir Cecil

J. B. Hurst states that royal assent was given to an act called the Cornwall Submarine Mines Act on August 2, 1858. This act declared, in section 2, that minerals acquired from mines and workings below low-water mark under the open sea adjacent to but not constituting part of the County of Cornwall were vested in the Queen as part of the soil and territorial possessions of the Crown. Parliament by this enactment committed itself to the dictum that the bed of the sea below low-water mark is vested in the Crown. Since the rights of the Crown were fixed prior to the time when existing rules of international law on such questions as the three-mile limit developed, the act established precedent and authority on matters related to the bed of the sea pertaining to pearl or chank fisheries, submarine cables, and tunnels.[179]

The origin of the Cornwall Submarine Mines Act is reported in the judgments of Lords Coleridge C.J. and Cockburn C.J., in *Rex* v. *Keyn*.[180] A controversy occurred between the Crown and the Duchy of Cornwall concerning ownership of minerals recovered from beneath the water on the coast of Cornwall. The minerals were obtained between high- and low-water mark, below low-water mark in tidal rivers and estuaries, and below low-water mark in the open sea. The question was referred to arbitration. The decision declared that the right to mines and minerals situated under the seashore between high- and low-water mark and under estuaries and tidal rivers below low-water mark in the County of Cornwall was vested in the Prince of Wales, "as part of the soil and territorial possessions of the Duchy of Cornwall," and that the right to all mines and minerals lying below low-water mark under the open sea adjacent to the County of Cornwall but not forming part of it was vested in Her Majesty the Queen. Sir John Patterson recommended that effect should be given to his award by legislation. Thereafter the bill was introduced and in 1858 became law as the Cornwall Submarine Mines Act. No rationale was stated for the decision that the minerals obtained from workings below low-water mark must belong to the Crown.[181]

Sir Cecil commented that Lord Coleridge and Lord Chief Justice Cockburn stated opposed views in the case; the former based his argument on the enactment of 1858 to substantiate his opinion that possessory territorial jurisdiction within the three-mile zone below low-water mark was vested in the Crown. Having access to all the proceedings in the arbitration and of the written arguments presented by both parties to the suit, Lord Coleridge stated in his judgment that the Crown's contention was based on the rationale that the *"fundus maris"* below "low-water mark belonged in property to the Crown."[182] The Duchy of Cornwall founded its dictum on the position that the bed of the sea belonged to the Prince as a right of the initial occupant, and therefore he possessed the mines under the bed of the sea. It would appear that Sir John Patterson regarded the right of the Crown to these minerals as a territorial right; that the property in the seabed was a vested right of the Crown, rather than mere sovereignty or jurisdictional right. His recommendation was inconsistent with the *res nullius* doctrine to the effect that the right to minerals acquired from below low-water mark is founded on seizure or occupation of a *res nullius*.[183] If the right of the Crown in the soil of the seabed below low-water mark is assumed to be a territorial right concerned with ownership of the soil, removed from a mere jurisdictional right, inquiry may be made as to the extent of such property rights and the relationship of the rights to the three-mile limit of territorial waters.

The rights of the Crown are shrouded in the earliest annals of the national history, while the three-mile limit of the extent of the marginal jurisdiction of the Crown is of modern origin. Its doctrine had its inception in Bynkershoek's *De Dominio Maris*, which was published in 1702. Decisions in early cases indicated that the rights of the Crown in the seabed must have existed as early as the thirteenth century. The proposition seems to be established that, at least within the three-mile zone, the seabed below low-water mark is territorial and the property of the sovereign.[184] Wider claims to jurisdiction apparently lapsed into desuetude.

In the nineteenth century additional claims to subsoil resources situated on the continental shelves involving underseas mines, often within the limit of territorial waters, were made by Australia, Canada, Chile, and Japan. These claims, together with those in England, were established upon the recognized right of a littoral state to occupy the subsoil beneath the high seas by mining installations located on land with extensions of equipment into the adjacent territorial sea. Therefore it may be asserted that particular claims by littoral states to the subsoil of the respective continental shelves during the nineteenth century were confined to underseas mines.[185]

Despite differences between the early claims to the resources of the seabed and subsoil and those of the mid-twentieth century the early claims were precursors of contemporary continental shelf declarations. Nineteenth-century claims and preceding ones observed the doctrine of the freedom of the seas because the methods of exploitation did not include high seas installations. Ships harvested sedentary fisheries, while mineral exploitation was an operation through tunnel systems originating on the landmass. However, certain enactments such as the British Colonial Act of 1811 prevented harvesting of sedentary fisheries and debarred other states from participation in extractions from the pearl banks.[186]

In contrast, the exploitation of the continental shelves at present, principally for oil, often necessitates the construction of installations, affixed permanently to the seabed and the subsoil of the shelf, which extend above the surface of the high seas. This necessarily involves certain interference with the free use of the seas by other states for navigational purposes, fishing privileges, cable and pipeline installations, scientific research, and other activities. Because of the possibility of interference by the littoral state, through its exploitation of the continental shelf, with the justifiable free use of the seas by other states, the International Law Commission's draft articles and the Geneva Convention on the Continental Shelf contain provisions preventing unjustifiable interference.[187]

In 1918 the United States, through its Department of State, manifested lack of interest in the continental shelf. An American citizen who had allegedly discovered oil in the Gulf of Mexico about forty miles from land inquired whether property or leasehold rights to a specific tract of ocean floor might be acquired as a protective title prior to drilling operations for the extraction of oil. The State Department replied that the United States possessed no jurisdiction over the ocean floor of the Gulf of Mexico beyond the territorial waters contiguous to the coast.[188] A changing American attitude toward the continental shelf was expressed during 1935, when the Copeland Bill passed the Senate, purporting to extend the jurisdiction of the United States as a protective measure against the encroachment of salmon fishing by the Japanese off the shore of Alaska. The Copeland Bill sought to extend the jurisdiction of the United States to "all the waters and submerged land adjacent to the coast of Alaska . . . and lying within the limits of the continental shelf having a depth of water of

100 fathoms, more or less." This bill was confined to senatorial action only. However, it served as a precursor of the Truman Proclamation of 1945 concerning fisheries and perhaps was instrumental in the formulation of contemporary continental shelf doctrine.[189]

The initial mid-twentieth century claim by states to the resources of the seabed and subsoil of the continental shelf in accord with the definition set forth in the Geneva Convention was the treaty between the United Kingdom and Venezuela of February 26, 1942, concerning submarine zones of the Gulf of Paria. The Treaty of Paria provided for the annexation of one-half of the submarine zone underlying the Gulf of Paria by the signatory states. This treaty was the beginning of certain international prescriptions relative to the continental shelf. However, the strongest impetus for the subsequent unilateral claims to the resources of the continental shelf was provided in 1945 by the Truman Proclamation, declaring that the United States considered the natural subsoil and seabed of the continental shelf contiguous to the United States as "appertaining to the United States, subject to its jurisdiction and control."[190]

The Truman Proclamation or Presidential Proclamation 2667, of September 28, 1945, with respect to natural resources of the subsoil and seabed of the continental shelf, stated that the government of the United States of America, being cognizant of the long-range world-wide need for additional sources of petroleum and other minerals, maintained the opinion that efforts to discover these resources should be encouraged, and that such resources should be made available. The pronouncement continued that competent experts held the view that such resources existed beneath many areas of the continental shelf off the coasts of the United States of America, and that utilization of the resources was practicable. The proclamation stated that recognized jurisdiction over these resources was necessary for conservation and rational utilization when they were developed. The exercise of jurisdiction over the natural resources of the subsoil and seabed of the continental shelf by the contiguous nation was deemed to be reasonable and just, since the area might be considered as an extension of the landmass of the coastal state and appurtenant to it. These resources are often a seaward projection of a pool or deposit located within the territory.[191] In view of these circumstances, the proclamation declared that natural resources of the subsoil and seabed of the continental shelf beneath the high seas but contiguous to the coasts of the United States appertained to the United States and was subject to its jurisdiction and control.[192] The proclamation attempts no enunciation regarding the width of the sea over which the continental shelf zone up to the hundred-fathom line extends; however, the distance is estimated to be up to 250 miles at certain points. The proclamation further declares that where an adjacent state shares the continental shelf, the boundary will be determined by the United States and the adjacent state "in accordance with equitable principles." This is in no way to affect the character of the waters above the continental shelf and the right to their free and unimpeded navigation.[193]

The Presidential Proclamation thus reserved only jurisdictional rights and control over the natural resources of the subsoil and seabed of the shelf, explicitly excluding the shelf waters, and designated such area as high seas, subject to the right of free navigation. In subsequent declarations of other states, however, claims were made to sovereignty and ownership over the seabed and subsoil, together with the waters over the shelf. Such claims constituted an extension of jurisdiction beyond the territorial sea in excess of the breadth of the contiguous zones. The official United States description of the area of the continental shelf was:

. . . almost as large as the area embraced in the Louisiana Purchase, which was 827,000 square miles and almost twice as large as the original 13 colonies which was 400,000 square miles. Along the Alaska coastline the shelf extends several hundred miles under the Bering Sea. On the Eastern coast of the United States the width of the shelf varies 20 miles to 250 miles, and along the Pacific coast it is from 1 to 50 miles wide.[194]

Thus, the Truman Proclamation issued a claim to a submarine area of greater magnitude than any previous historical claim, and one which, because of progress in technological developments in the United States, made possible the recovery of mineral resources from undersea zones. The legal foundation of the United States claims is apparently based on a valid occupation of the shelf by the coastal state.

Because of the great area of the continental shelf, there was only a very slight analogy between the vast general claims and exclusive claims of control over limited zones of the seabed beyond the territorial sea. Restricted claims relied upon the occupation of the seabed as a *res nullius* or upon some traditional or quasi-prescriptive title or some particularized regional community of interest (e.g., the pearl fisheries in the Persian Gulf).[195]

Assertions which followed the proclamation indicated that a new principle of customary international law had probably evolved which ascribed to the littoral state exclusive rights for purposes of exploration or exploitation of the resources of the seabed and subsoil of the continental shelf.[196] An opponent of the emergent principle stated, however, that the doctrine of the continental shelf lacked the "hard lineaments or the definitive status of an established rule of international law," and that the diverse acts and proclamations of a limited number of states affirming sovereign rights over shelf zones failed, even by recurrence of declarations, to contribute to the establishment of a customary rule of international law.[197]

In instances where such claims are tantamount to the appropriation of, or to exclusive jurisdiction over, the waters overlying the shelf, they are violative of rules governing the recognized principle of the freedom of the seas. However, claims which in the beginning were illegal may be converted to valid titles by assent, acquiescence, recognition, or on a *tu quoque* basis, which by degrees of gradualism leads to an estoppel.[198]

The Truman Doctrine became the subject of a treaty, the Convention on the Continental Shelf, resulting from a report of the subcommittee of the General Assembly of the United Nations on the "Law of the Sea" in 1956. In 1964 some thirty nations had formally accepted the principles, and many other participating nations recognize certain principles contained in the convention. In general, under international law, this doctrine is considered in force and effective, although boundaries of national claims are subject to variance in interpretation.[199]

This treaty established sovereignty of the contiguous nation over operations for mineral exploitation in the seabed; the treaty provides that explorative activities shall not interfere with rights to navigation, fishing, and other justified uses. Therefore, the right to explore on a continental shelf is obtainable by the execution of a legal document from a given nation granting the right subject to certain conditions.[200]

The Geneva Convention did not confer to the coastal state sovereignty over any portion of the high seas. The state may merely exercise sovereign rights for exploratory purposes and exploitation of the natural resources of the continental shelf. The convention does not affect the legal status of the waters of the high seas or of the airspace above these waters.[201]

It is assumed that the exploitation of mineral resources by ocean mining will be subject to a legal regime. In considerations of the exact nature of such a legal regime the initial question would be whether the resources were already under the regime of the continental shelf. If the resources are subject to this regime, the coastal state would have jurisdictional claims over them.

As to the developmental aspects of ocean mining, it has been stated that inquiry will be necessary as to the method of acquiring exclusive legal rights for exploitation of the mineral resources of the deep sea. Producers will necessarily require exclusive rights to justify the economic responsibility; an entrepreneur must be assured of a degree of security of investment over an adequate area and of sufficient duration for a productive return.[202]

Needs of the mineral industry are complex; certain rights are essential in connection with explorations and exploitation of such minerals. The first essential right of the mineral industry would be the right to mine an ore deposit if one is discovered in exploratory efforts. This right involves the removal of the valuable minerals and certain necessary disturbance of the environment of the mineral deposit. The right to mine must accrue at an appropriate time to exclusive utilization by one party—in usual procedure, the discoverer of the deposit. The tenure of the discoverer must be attached to an area of adequate size and for a sufficient period of time to justify operational costs, to amortize his investment, and to enable him to receive an economic benefit in profit for the enterprise.[203] Other legal rights required for mining industries are rights of initial and continued access during entire operations; means of transportation on, above, or below the ocean; the use of suitable space for necessary ancillary purposes such as treatment areas; and disposal of waste products. These rights are required for mining operations both on land and in oceanic areas. As in land mining projects, the time involved and acquisition costs of these rights will reflect upon incentives to explore and the economic benefits of mining activities in the ocean. Extractive industries engaged in the production of solid minerals have diminutive metal deposits for operational purposes in comparison with petroleum companies. Also the predictability of occurence of great metal deposits in given formations and structures is more limited in the case of hard minerals than in that of petroleum discoveries. Post-discovery expenditure in solid mineral production is accelerated until actual production. Currently, the establishment of shafts from the ocean down into rock formations of the shelf and the mining of deposits would seem to be impracticable, economically hazardous, and technically difficult, and costs are inhibitory to profitable explorations.[204] However, with increased demands for mineral resources, improved technical competence, and diminished land reserves, it is predictable that ocean mining will be accelerated despite existing obstacles.

Computed on present cost structures and present technological capability, established reserves of many major minerals indicate only a ten- to twenty-year supply at present projections of estimated consumption. Mining operations for solid minerals on the sea floor will be contingent upon solutions of complex technological problems. Unique risks in ocean mining are also recognized.[205]

Exploitation of minerals on the ocean floor of the deep abyss, seaward of the continental margin, will be economically impracticable until there is scarcity of those minerals at the less expensive sources on the continental margin and exposed continental land areas.

Petroleum and Gas Exploration and Exploitation

Petroleum and gas are the most economically profitable minerals which are currently extracted from the sea floor. Offshore production is from the continental shelf; however, operations are extending continuously to greater depths. Recovery of oil from continental slopes and deeper areas of the continental margin is possible. However, exploitation of petroleum at substantially greater oceanic depths may be deferred for decades because of excessive production costs from deeper water areas.[206]

It is estimated that during the forthcoming thirty-year period, petroleum demands will far exceed total production in the world to date. A major portion of the needed petroleum for world consumption will be located offshore.

To supply unprecedented consumption demands, new areas must be located for potential petroleum development. Certain experts in the field are of the opinion that the most significant source of potential petroleum resources is to be found in the continental shelf. Already the petroleum industry has been engaged for two decades in the successful exploration and exploitation of this area, in developmental efforts for new sources of liquid fuel.[207]

Initial interest in continental shelf petroleum resources was aroused when investigations revealed the extension beyond the water's edge of the productive limits of many coastal oilfields originating on land. The development of such an extension of petroleum production occurred before the beginning of the twentieth century off the coast of California. This discovery and other early extensions were developed by wells drilled from wharves, or directionally from land areas. During 1947, discovery wells were drilled from a platform in the Gulf of Mexico at locations twelve miles from shore in water twenty feet in depth. The successful efforts of these early marine explorations resulted in approximately 250 oil and gas fields on the continental shelf of the United States. Of this number approximately 90 percent are found in the Gulf of Mexico in water areas up to a depth of 300 feet. Many of these drilling sites are situated offshore at distances as great as 100 miles.[208] Petroleum explorations are continuing. Exploration in the United States is at present confined to shallow portions of the continental shelf along the East, West, and Gulf Coasts. With future successful domestic marine resources exploitations it is expected that activities will move toward deeper areas of the approximately 875,000 square miles of the continental shelf of the United States, including Alaska. Exploration may extend to the continental slope comprised of approximately 300,000 square miles with depths of 6,500 feet. Further industrial drilling for gas and oil will be conducted in water depths of 1,000 feet, and later full-scale pressure-controlled drilling will be done in locations of 3,000 feet. Drilling capacity in 4,800 feet of water has been demonstrated in the Gulf and the Pacific by the utilization of dynamically positioned surface floating vessels. Petroleum and gas explorations are now in progress offshore in some forty countries; important discoveries have been made in offshore areas of such countries as Mexico, Trinidad, Brazil, Norway, Dahomey, Nigeria, Cabinda (Angola), Australia, Formosa, Mainland China, and certain countries bordering the North Sea.[209] Developments during 1968 proved wider areas to be subject to economic utilization both by lateral exploitation of new locations of the ocean shelves and by vertical drilling in deeper waters.

Drilling operations at various depths in the marine environment and at varied distances from shore have been the subject of divergent views. Drilling on the continental shelf requires space for exploitations by the mineral industry; generally a stationary position is required. Usually a mineral-producing installation is immobile. Installations may not be changed to accommodate transitory sea traffic; unique techniques are necessary. Until the immediate past, explosives have been employed to make geologic studies of structures beneath the ocean floor. In initial operations, floating platforms are used for drills on the floor of the sea. Later stationary platforms are affixed to the sea floor. The presence of such platforms may obstruct other justified uses of the sea and consequently again raises the issue of freedom of the seas.[210]

Conclusion

The appraisal by committees of the National Academy of Engineering of 1969 in *An Oceanic Quest* stated that currently exploitation of marine mineral resources, including oil and gas, is essentially restricted to the continental shelf. Petroleum and natural gas are the principal products. In 1967 the sea floor adjacent to the United States yielded $1.7 billion worth of petroleum, natural gas, and sulfur. The appraisal expressed the need for information on abundance, composition, and distribution of deep-sea deposits, together with an evaluation of their utility, as a basis for management and jurisdictional considerations.

Diverse scientific and engineering investigations are essential for the expedition of discovery of ocean mineral resources. Physiographic mapping and reconnaissance geological-geophysical exploration of the continental margin can serve as basic information for study and prospecting for marine industry. Accurate delineation of the continental margin and the deep ocean is essential as a prerequisite in ultimate establishment of regimes and jurisdictional claims. Also, realization of mineral resource potential may be facilitated by exploration of the deep-sea floor and small ocean basins. Fundamental studies of seafloor contours, sedimentation, and processes are needed. Knowledge is necessary concerning the development of mineral-recovery systems, prediction of surface oceanic conditions and atmospheric conditions, and general characteristics of the seabed.[211]

Knowledge concerning mineral deposits on the continental slope and continental shelf is fragmentary. There is diversity of opinion in the community of nations relative to political and geopolitical positions. Moreover, misconceptions abound regarding the width of the legal continental shelf. Therefore it has been advocated that support should be given to the resolution proposed in 1966 by the Committee on the Law of the Sea Section on International Comparative Law of the American Bar Association. This Committee on the Law of the Sea urged that the United States government review the issues involved by consultation with representatives of the association possessing competence in the area of international law, with scientific and technical experts, and with leaders in American industry affiliated with oceanic development, prior to formulation of policy vis-à-vis other nations in regard to resources of the sea not governed by existing legal principles. It reiterated the need for clarification of the question of where sovereignty over minerals located on the shelf ends and where the area of the deep ocean floor in which minerals are unallocated begins. It is predictable that in future years the deep ocean floor will require international regulation; such regulation should be based upon full knowledge of scientific data and a clear exposition of existing treaty law.[212]

CHAPTER FOUR

COMMUNITY INTERESTS
VERSUS EXCLUSIVE STATE POLICIES

GRADUALLY, freedom of the high seas gained recognition in the practice of states as a general legal principle; however, it became apparent that the doctrine was subject to politico-economic realities similar to those which occasioned its inception.

Even though coastal states fully recognized the freedom of the high seas, there was general reluctance, even unwillingness, to agree that the free seas extended to the actual shoreline of respective states. Essential basic needs of coastal states to assert jurisdiction over waters adjacent to land territorial limits resulted in the crystallization of the doctrine of the territorial sea and the principle of the contiguous zone of the high seas. The shore state is legal sovereign of the territorial sea area; beyond this zone the coastal state can exercise a limited jurisdiction in a contiguous zone of the high sea. The special jurisdiction is recognized for purposes of law enforcement, national security, and control of fishery rights. The existence of these zones is accepted by the community of nations; however, there is disparity of views relative to the width of the zones.[1]

The differentiation between community interests and exclusive state policies is associated with geomorphological data concerning the territorial sea, the continental shelf, and the rights of exploitation of mineral resources by the coastal state. The physical characteristics of the shelf have been employed by jurists in the application of the doctrine of propinquity. The principle of contiguity was embodied in the Proclamation of President Truman;[2] in the fourth paragraph the shelf was interpreted as an extension of the landmass of the coastal state and appurtenant to it. Also, in the phraseology of the Mexican and Argentinian decrees, and later the Peruvian decree, the shelf was regarded as a single morphological and geologic unity with the continental area. The significant criterion was the rule of continuity. According to this rule, the shelf was in fact the submarine continuation of the territory above water.

Certain authorities support the view that by the principle of propinquity, the geographical contours of the location would determine the primary right of the shore state to procurable resources within the submarine area. However, an opposing view questioned the validity of applying one science to another; in geology, the fact that the shelf is beneath the sea in no manner affects the unity of the continent and the shelf, while in law, the legal status of the sea differs from that of the landmass.[3] The term "continental shelf," therefore, has both a geological and a legal connotation.[4] The acceptance of the geological conception of the shelf with its variances concerning depths, breadths, and distances would, in the opinion of one authority,[5] lead to interminable conflicts, for clear concepts and discernible limits are necessary for certification of legal titles to mineral resources.

In addition to geomorphological considerations relative to the continental shelf, it should be mentioned that traditionally international law has long served in the achievement of equilibrium between special exclusive claims of coastal states and the inclusive claims of all other states in the international community. While historically the world ocean was at one period claimed for the exclusive utilization of certain states, concern for the general interest of the entire community of states ultimately resulted in the liberation of the greater oceanic expanses for relatively unencumbered uses by all states. Although consensus evolved that states were denied the exercise of comprehensive authority beyond a relatively narrow margin of such waters, it was readily recognized that the occasional exercise of certain coastal authority in areas beyond the belt was essential for protection of special interests. Thus, through interactive experiences of particular claims and general community recognition or rejection, a body of principles effected a compromise between coastal state demands and noncoastal state claims. The resultant was effective internationalization in the common interest of the oceans of the world.[6]

Proceeding from historic and geological conceptions of the shelf to contemporary aspects of community interests and exclusive state policies, during the twentieth century unparalleled claims have been made concerning exclusive authority of states over extended oceanic areas.

Competitive and frequently conflicting interests of generally inclusive claims of all other states involve equality of access to all areas of the world ocean, prohibition of exclusive dominion of sea areas for the acquisition of influence, public order upon the high seas, encouragement of rational conservation of wealth, productive uses of the sea and its resources, the establishment and preservation of safety, navigational freedom, the allocation of the advantages available in oceanic areas, the preservation of the oceans as an essential means of transportation, communication, and exploration and exploitation of marine resources.[7]

Rights and Demands of the Coastal States to Use Their Resources

DEMANDS IN GENERAL

After World War II certain coastal states exercised new extended claims beyond territorial waters. These claims, although vigorously opposed, resulted in enlargement of the area of internal waters and expanded the entire water area over which the coastal states exercised the most extensive authority. The most controversial of recent issues indicated an alteration in perspectives; the questions involved the extension of the territorial sea to protect numerous particular interests of claimant states. Moreover, increased demands were initiated concerning the occasional exercise of exclusive authority in adjacent areas of the sea, the contiguous zones.[8] A number of states are currently pressing claims to obtain exclusive authority for the exploitation of oil located in the continental shelves.[9] While present demands are confined to relatively restricted areas of the shelf, it is foreseeable that exclusive claims will be extended seaward into areas of the open sea, as exploitation of mineral resources is made feasible through technological innovations.[10]

Concurrently with the increased variety and complexity of demands for exclusive authority, comprehensive efforts have been made to stabilize diverse economic demands and to allocate existing and potential resources to the peoples of the international community. In accord with these objectives, international governmental conferences have been convened, international private entrepreneurial experts have participated, and yet consideration of the overall interests of the community and the particular interests of respective claimants has failed to achieve definitive clarification of the issues. Even the notable prolonged contributions of the International Law Commission proved to be inadequate to define extended national interest in juxtaposition with factors of common interest.[11]

Demands of states adjacent to the sea embody protective measures and power to control access to territorial bases for regulatory activities and maintenance of order in adjacent waters. Additional interests of coastal states include economic welfare, wealth, exclusive control over distribution of resources, and preservation of internal asset-producing processes. Other general controls include inspection, quarantine, pollution control, scientific exploration, research, and exploitation of mineral resources.[12]

For the accommodation and preservation of coastal and noncoastal interests, flexible prescriptive rights have emerged through centuries of evolution. The exclusive interests of the coastal state are formulated in well-known terminology: "internal waters," "territorial sea," "contiguous zone," "continental shelf," and "hot pursuit." The prescriptions honor both comprehensive and particular claims affirmed by coastal states which may interfere with inclusive claims with regard to navigational freedom and fishery rights. These prescriptive rights are those which are usually categorized under the general title of "freedom of the seas."[13]

A series of exclusive claims by states resulted in controversy and conjecture over the legal status of the seabed and subsoil of offshore areas located beyond territorial limits. These claims were motivated by the feasibility of marine explorations and the exploitability of immense mineral resources beneath the seas. Apprehension has been expressed lest efforts to protect claims to more inclusive uses of the sea may in fact maximize assertions of absolutistic doctrines of freedom of the sea and thereby minimize or neglect the complementary portion of the law which is protective of the exclusive interests of coastal states, and may even go to the extreme of denying on occasion the accommodation of competitive inclusive uses.[14]

The methods employed by states for the assertion of claims to authority over areas of the oceans of the world include unilateral declarations and multilateral agreements. Participants in processes of claim include states, international governmental organizations, individuals, and associations. The general objectives of claimant states include characteristic benefits of power, wealth, scientific research, and exploration. General demands are related to specific claims to uses of the oceans or oceanic areas for transportation, laying of cables or pipelines, the extraction of minerals, and other activities. The many assertive comprehensive claims may on occasion interfere with given special uses. There is a great range of potential interferences between various uses and users of oceans. The comprehensiveness of the claim and the geographical area in which the claim is asserted are of significance; the state may make comprehensive claims to "internal waters" which are complete and absolute, in the absence of a contrary agreement. Beyond question the exclusiveness of rights in the territorial sea has at all periods been accepted by the majority of states to the advantage of the coastal state, with the exception of acknowledged restrictions necessary to protect other existing interests or rights of other states. The derivation of the right of exclusiveness has been the subject of debate as to whether exclusiveness originated as a property right, sovereignty, dominion, *imperium*, or jurisdiction. The rights of the state in the territorial sea are analogous to equivalent rights in its territorial dry land.[15]

Certain claimants have made monopolistic inordinate claims under the pretext of increased protection for and enlargement of their exclusive interests; such claims have served to encourage similar encroachments by other claimants. This provinciality leads to acquisition of enormous ocean areas, under extensive sovereign authority, to the exclusion of or at least interference with previous inclusive uses. One familiar exercise of sovereign authority is the right of exclusive disposition by the coastal state of mineral resources in the territorial margin.[16]

Relative to the judicial status of the natural resources of this area, the Report on Territorial Waters which was presented to the League of Nations Committee of Experts for the Progressive Codification of International Law stated that by virtue of the right of dominion by the littoral state over the entire area of its territorial waters, it possesses for itself and its citizenry the exclusive right of ownership over the riches of the sea. This right includes the fauna found in such waters, together with all that may be found above or below the subsoil of the territorial sea. This concept of the right of the coastal state over the resources existing in or to be found in its territorial sea is a logical extension of exclusiveness which is the dominative distinction of the area.[17] Resources existing in the subsoil and those permanently attached to the ocean floor are subject to the exclusive right of use and exploitation of the littoral state.[18]

Obviously, the territorial sea is a reservoir of rights for coastal states with attendant obligations and responsibilities; therefore, it may be reiterated that unjustified extreme provincialism by unilateral extensive claims beyond traditional territorial seas is a disadvantage for the international community, especially in view of the fact that the contiguous zone is available as a shield for all reasonable interests of the coastal state without its resorting to the hazardous intrusion into the inclusive general use of the sea. Such nationalistic interpretations constitute a jeopardy to the internationalization of the waters of the world ocean which traditionally has well served the community of nations.[19]

SPECIFIC UNILATERAL PROCLAMATIONS

As we have said, a number of maritime states asserted unilateral claims to exclusive jurisdiction or control over marine resources of the continental shelf and certain offshore zones. Efforts were exerted to vindicate these claims by geographical definitions of the shelf and by considerations of national security. Initially the purpose of unilateral declarations was for reservation to the littoral state of such oil deposits as might be located within the scope of the shelf, since advances in technological capability had made feasible the extraction of petroleum deposits in the area. The claims were asserted in terms adequate to include all minerals and nonmineral resources.[20] These claims varied in range; the proclamation issued by the President of the United States in September, 1945, retained only rights of "jurisdiction and control" over natural marine resources of the subsoil and seabed of the shelf; an express stipulation in the proclamation left unimpaired the characterization of the waters above the shelf as high seas as well as the right of free navigation. However, subsequent unilateral instruments of declaration by certain other states made exaggerated claims to sovereignty and ownership over the seabed and subsoil, including the water areas overlying the shelf. Obviously, these claims constituted an extension of jurisdictional authority or sovereign powers beyond the limits of the territorial sea and for a distance in excess of the width of the contiguous zones.[21]

These extended claims are conducive to conflicting uses of the submarine areas. It is foreseeable that mineral exploitations in the seabed and subsoil may constitute an activity incompatible with traditional uses of the oceans. A great number of recommendations have been presented concerning specificity of balanced interests of navigation, flight, fishing rights, cable pipelines, and scientific investigations in relationship with new claims.[22]

The Truman Proclamation and succeeding declarations are predicated on the supposition that the coastal state can exercise rights over the continental shelf contiguous to its territory. These unilateral declarations, however, reveal various concepts as to the characteristics and extent of these rights.[23] It will be recalled that the Truman Proclamation regarded the natural resources of the subsoil and seabed of the shelf below the high seas but adjacent to the coastal area of the United States as appertaining to the United States and subject to its "jurisdiction and control." When other states declared "sovereignty" over the continental shelf or made claims that the given area was within state territory, there were contentions that the United States had exercised more restraint in its claims. Other interpretations minimized the distinction between the various claims as to jurisdiction and control and of assertions of sovereignty. Professor Gidel has stated that the Truman position was not a declaration of sovereignty but rather a contained and specialized right with regard to certain zones beyond the extent of the territorial sea. Sir Hersch Lauterpacht could make no differentiation between exclusive jurisdiction and control and sovereignty and stated that the proclamations have "in law and in fact assumed sovereignty," subject to legal impositions recognized by international law and to reasonable interpretations of the principle of freedom of the seas.[24]

The extent of the coastal state's claims over the continental shelf was the subject of debate in the Fourth Committee of the 1958 Geneva Conference on the Law of the Sea. The discussion revealed that division of opinion continued regarding terms of the various unilateral declarations pertaining to the continental shelf.[25]

One category of countries including the Argentine Republic and Mexico proclaimed sovereignty over the epicontinental sea and the continental shelf. Similar, but more extensive, were the declarations of Peru, Chile, Costa Rica, and Uruguay. The Senate and Chamber of Deputies of Nicaragua adopted a Declaration under Article 2 of the Constitution of 1948 stating that the continental shelf is that portion of the territory beneath the sea up to a depth of two hundred meters, and that in instances where the continental shelf extends to the coast of another state, the point of demarcation should be ascertained by agreement on an equitable basis. Certain coastal states declared complete sovereignty over the shelf by reason of geographical definition and the fact of appurtenance of the area to the mainland. Honduras decreed that the submarine platform or continental and insular shelf and the water above the area in both the Atlantic and Pacific Oceans, whatever its depth or however far it extends, should form part of the national land territory of Honduras. Therefore, the coastal state possessing sovereignty over the land had a vested right of sovereignty over the continental shelf.[26] Unilateral claims have also been made by Panama, Guatemala, El Salvador, Brazil, Ecuador, the Dominican Republic, Venezuela, and others.[27]

Certain delegations rejected the conclusion that the coastal state possessed sovereignty over the continental shelf and regarded its right as restricted to exploration and exploitation of certain natural resources of the shelf.[28]

Under the 1958 Convention the coastal state does not possess unlimited sovereign rights over the continental shelf, but has rights of exploration and exploitation of the natural resources of the area. The convention also provided for the preservation and reaffirmation of the legal status as high seas of the waters above the shelf.

It has been said that the excessive claims in unilateral proclamations to sovereignty over submarine areas have been distorted for the

purpose of extending pretensions to sovereignty over the high seas as
such or the exclusive exploitation of the resources of the seabed and
subsoil of the deep sea. Such assumptions of title over submarine
areas with disproportionate claims to sovereignty over the high seas
are obviously contrary to international law. The test of reasonableness
and of common interests must be considered in the exploitation of
submarine resources by the coastal state.[29] In previous practice, states
were free to utilize the oceans in accommodation with other uses.
Thus through the exercise of judicious concepts many types of uses
were simultaneously accommodated, thereby precluding state license
to participate in activities which might be detrimental in their effects
upon the interests of other states.[30]

SAFEGUARDS FOR COMMUNITY INTERESTS

Of paramount significance in the codification of the regime of the
continental shelf was the assurance that the exclusive rights of the
coastal states should be exercised in a manner which observed the
general rights of states, the community interests, in the use of the
waters overlying the shelf. Due to the diversity of possible uses of
such waters, some degree of interference was unavoidable; however
the 1958 Convention endeavored to achieve a rational equilibrium
between these varied uses and users by adopting certain safeguards.
The primary safeguard affected the preservation of the status of the
superjacent waters as high seas. The provision in Article 3 stated:[31]

> The rights of the coastal state over the continental shelf do not affect the
> legal status of the superjacent waters as high seas, or that of the airspace above
> those waters.

The following safeguard confined the "sovereign rights" of the coastal
state to "the purpose of exploring and exploiting its natural resources."
Provision is made in Article 5(1) that

> The exploration of the continental shelf and exploitation of its natural re-
> sources must not result in any unjustifiable interference with navigation, fishing
> or the conservation of the living resources of the sea, nor result in any interference
> with fundamental oceanographic or other scientific research carried out with the
> intention of open publication.[32]

Also, the Geneva Convention on the High Seas provided that the freedom of the seas "shall be exercised by all States with reasonable regard to the interests of other states in their exercise of the freedom of the high seas."[33]

The principle of freedom of the seas can be effectively realized only by observance of reasonable regard for the general interests of other states, including the utilization and conservation of the sea's resources; unrestricted exploitation of marine resources is insupportable and unjustifiable under traditional concepts of international law. The establishment of rational rules must be effected for the insurance of protective legal rights applicable to the coastal state and the legal rights of other legitimate users of the high seas.[34] Inclusive interests of all states have been accommodated through traditional, historic order of the oceans with the exclusive interests of coastal states.[35] Reciprocal interests require the recognition of mutual restraints in unilateral assertions of sovereignty over the superjacent high seas and the reconciliation of conflicting uses as a proper safeguard of community interests.[36]

In general, we may say that in decades prior to the mid-twentieth century freedom of the seas was interpreted to mean the freedom of each state to utilize the oceans on a basis of reciprocity or accommodation with other users, rather than state license to participate in activities irrespective of possible effects upon uses by other states. Since 1945, however, strident nationalism has been the motivation for heuristic debate concerning state competence to extend seaward claims far in excess of traditional state claims. The indulgence in tergiversation by certain states has served to obscure the relativity of uses and interests of other nation-states.[37] Repercussions inevitably followed such a course, affecting not only the long-accepted doctrine of freedom of the seas but also rights of exploitation and conservation of the natural resources of the sea. Therefore, it may be appropriate to enumerate previous efforts toward regulatory measures concerning such resources.

The earliest effort to establish an international body to consider the subject was made at the Stockholm International Conference of 1899. This conference recommended a research program to serve as a foundation for ultimate international legislation. Subsequently, two conferences were held, at Oslo in 1901 and at Copenhagen in 1902. The Copenhagen Conference created an "International Permanent

Council for the Exploration of the Sea," which met at regular intervals in the Danish capital. The council concentrated its study on biological and hydrographical conditions of the sea, together with questions concerning the regulation and administration of fisheries through international agreement. In 1919, a similar organization was established for the Mediterranean. A North-American Commission was created in 1921 for fishery research pertaining to the Pacific and Atlantic oceans. This Commission had representatives from Canada, Newfoundland, the United States, and France. The scientific studies conducted by these organizations have assisted materially in promoting a knowledge of the resources of the sea. These contributions constituted preliminary bases for regulations concerning marine products.[38]

The Institute of International Law has made notable contributions, especially in 1937 at its Luxemburg Conference, when a recommendation was adopted to the effect that interested governments of states should, by internationally organized scientific research, develop the study of questions related to the preservation of the wealth of the sea, with particular interest in the marine fauna. The study was directed against certain abuses and destructive practices hazardous to sea life and was also a protest against unrestrained emission of oil and other harmful substances. Protective measures were urged for the rational preservation of the wealth of the sea.[39] Furthermore, the Committee of Experts appointed by the League of Nations for the codification of international law reported in 1927 that the problem of the exploitation of the products of the sea should be a subject of regulation by international agreement.[40] However, this proposal failed to materialize.

The unfinished work of the Committee of Experts was undertaken by the International Law Commission in 1951 under the aegis of the United Nations Organization. In its report of July 4, 1956, the commission set forth the inadequacy of existing law and international agreements concerning protection of fauna from predatory exploitation and extermination.[41] Coastal states had no effective means of resistance to the irrational exploitation of marine natural resources by foreign nationals, when prodigality in harvesting products of the sea rendered a state destitute of certain of these resources. Such abusive actions were conducive to friction and constituted a motivation for state unilateral action for self-protection. Measures of self-protection by states have in some instances led to exaggerated exclusion of foreign nationals in disregard of existing law.[42]

At the United Nations Conference on the Law of the Sea at Geneva held February 24 to April 29, 1958, the entire law of the sea was considered, while at the Hague Conference in 1930 the territorial sea had been the one topic under discussion. Since the breadth of the territorial sea, as well as new fishing claims, had been left undetermined by the 1958 Conference, the convening of a new conference to resolve these problems was justified. Therefore, a resolution was adopted on December 10, 1958, by the General Assembly authorizing a second conference on the law of the sea. In accordance with this resolution the secretary-general was requested to convoke such a conference in March or April, 1960.[43]

The proceedings of the respective conferences indicate that the development and codification of the international law of the sea have been directed in conformity with systematic and comprehensive plans, in the formation of which representatives of interested nations have been included. Pertinent drafts based upon technical and other data have usually been prepared and submitted by authoritative legal bodies. For example, the International Law Commission based its draft on the conservation of the living resources of the sea, issued at its seventh session in 1955, on certain conclusions of the Rome Conference. Also, the decision made at Ciudad Trujillo concerning exploitation of the natural resources of the sea included scientific, technical, and economic factual data. Moreover, in consideration of coordinative measures between the United Nations and the Organization of American States, the International Law Commission at its eighth session (1956) modified its 1953 draft on the "continental shelf" to incorporate relevant conclusions reached on the topic by the Inter-American Specialized Conference. The two organizations considered various aspects of the juridical regime of the sea—the regime in its entirety. The General Assembly of the United Nations, in acknowledgement of the "unity of the topic," adopted it as a foundational plan for its agenda. At the Caracas Conference the Organization of American States further amplified the idea of the unity of problems related to the sea.[44] Earlier resolutions of the General Assembly referred to the geographical and juridical unity of various marine areas, yet the interrelationship of aspects was omitted except in one instance. However, the acknowledgement of inextricable relationships is necessary to a consideration of problems emerging on the use and conservation of marine resources. Juridical, economic, social, and scientific aspects are significant in formulating the modern regime of the sea. These factors applied to submarine areas led to the recognition of the exclusive right of coastal states to exploitation of their seabed and subsoil. Economic and social interests are essentially the factors which will ultimately determine equitable legal protection for marine resources.[45]

Economic interests and legal problems concerning the harvesting of mineral resources of the deep sea have notable similarities and analogous relationships with certain fisheries operations, in that both enterprises represent major capital investments in mobile recovery equipment. The miners' capital investment involves not only the recovery system but the deposit as well. Some fifteen characteristics of a deposit of manganese nodules may affect the economics of mining the deposit. The miner, therefore, requires a legal regime which may grant exclusive rights for developing and mining the deposit. Such laws are nonexistent at present.[46]

EXISTING INTERNATIONAL PROCEDURES

Officials of nation-states have long been regarded as the most significant decision-makers in the law of the sea; it is foreseeable that with accelerated use of the sea the representatives of all states will participate in projecting adequate legal prescriptions or in the modification of old juridical prescriptions for attempted solutions of developing problems. However, it is to be expected that nations possessing advanced technological competence for exploitation will exert a major influence on decisions.[47]

Participation in authoritative decisions by international governmental organizations is of more recent origin and has resulted in noteworthy contributions. Notable in such formulative efforts was the concerted effective force of the United Nations in convening the most significant international conference ever held to codify international law, which formulated the Geneva Conventions on the law of the sea.[48] It is doubtful that such a conference with representation from some eighty-six nations could have been successfully convened in the absence of such an international organization. A specialized agency, the Inter-government Maritime Consultative Organization, is entirely concerned with maritime affairs.[49] Certain specialized agencies such as the United Nations Educational, Scientific and Cultural Organization (UNESCO) and the Food and Agriculture Organization are actively employed in ocean research and experimentation or in stimulating international direction to such activities. The Intergovernmental Conference on Oceanographic Research convened in 1960 recommended the establishment of an Intergovernmental Oceanographic Commission to function within UNESCO with the objective of concentrating efforts by states and international bodies and arranging cooperative endeavors having more permanent status. Also, the International Telecommunications Union and the World Meterological Organization have restricted competences relating to the oceans.[50]

Almost without exception, all specialized agencies of the United Nations are concerned with oceanic pursuits. Also, certain regional organizations are involved in marine programs, as are non-United Nations bodies such as fisheries commissions, together with bodies of a nongovernmental nature. It may be noted parenthetically that the initial comprehensive investigatory efforts concerning the oceans occurred as a segment of the International Geophysical Year established by the International Union of Geodesy and Physics in 1957. This successful venture led to the creation of the Special Committee on Oceanic Research (SCOR), which organized a study of the Indian Ocean. Later, in 1960, the United Nations Educational, Scientific and Cultural Organization established the Intergovernmental Oceanographic Commission (IOC). The commission has enlarged its original scope to include problems of marine pollution, assistance to emerging nations, legal aspects of oceanic research, and exploitation of marine resources.[51]

Regional bodies such as the North Atlantic Treaty Organization (NATO) and the Organization of American States maintain an interest in research and developmental aspects of exploitation of marine resources. Fisheries commissions are generally organized on a regional basis related to specific problems.

International bodies have participated in decision-making, together with private associations and national and international entities; these groups have long participated in the influencing of various official representatives. Even certain private individuals may have significant influence in processes of decision because of force of circumstances or through intellectual contributions.[52] A variety of organizations operate outside the formalities of governmental functions. For example, in the scientific field the Special Committee on Oceanic Research of the International Council of Scientific Unions is the paramount coordinating instrumentality for the world's scientists in functionary capacities, serving as advisor to the Intergovernmental Oceanographic Commission. Also, multinational industrial companies may be regarded as international organizations having direct interest in the oceans.[53]

PRESENT LACK OF SAFEGUARDS IN THE HIGH SEAS

Thus international and regional organizations have a wide variety of purposes and interests in the oceanic domain. One predominant characteristic prevails, however, in all bodies: they may and do influence decision-making but lack effective regulatory powers as well as powers of enforcement. (Even fishery commissions are fundamentally intergovernmental consultative and collaborative mechanisms lacking authority to enforce decisions.)[54]

Therefore certain nation-states, attempting to rectify present stultifying dilemmas concerning the lack of regulatory measures and enforcement capabilities of existing international organizations, decry the lack of safeguards in the high seas, the lack of uniformity concerning the breadth of the territorial sea, and ambiguities relative to the extent of continental shelves. They advocate clarification of rights of the coastal state; the terminal extension of the continental shelf; competitive practices in fishing and conservation; reassertion of freedom for all nations to engage in scientific research; and national security agreements concerning controls for military uses. Of great significance is the essential decision concerning the exploitation and conservation of marine resources. For every nation these questions and the formulations of policy are complex. Equitable laws for resources would include financial and economic considerations, orderly exploitation, possible influence on the market of the international community, effect upon widely varied activities in the sea, total global interests, peace, order, general welfare, foreign trade, aid, and development.[55] No agreement exists as to who owns the seabed and subsoil. The resources of the seabed can be exploited only in coastal waters by coastal states; legal confirmation of this right to resources by the coastal state operates in exclusion of other nations. In future develop-

ments legal questions will arise concerning the production of petroleum and harvesting of manganese in distances beyond coastal waters.
The legal ownership of the minerals and their distribution will be
questioned, and also whether extractive rights are subject to community approval.[56]

WHY NEW LEGAL SAFEGUARDS ARE NEEDED

The necessity for devising an international agency, body, or institution for the orderly development of an oceanic legal regime has
been reiterated by various authorities. Regarding fisheries and mineral
resources, it is said that international control and regulation will be
essential to insure performance and enforcement of agreements ultimately reached concerning natural resources. These agreements may
be formulated within a wide spectrum of minor international licensing
authority, to the extremity of ownership of the ocean floors with regulations relating to use, limitation of entry, and revenue distributions.[57]

Law for the deep sea should lend opportunity and encouragement
for the harvesting of resources of the sea with adequate protection for
participants. Equitable provisions should be observed to lessen causes
for disputes and to bring about amicable settlements if disagreements
occur. Various interests should be considered—that of the nation which
recovers the minerals, especially a nation-state claiming rights in
definite areas of the sea, and that of the world community. Other
justified uses should be considered: navigation, fishing, military uses,
scientific research, exploration, and recreation. The law should be
flexible to provide for potential interests; it should be tolerable to
nations generally to encourage compliance and to reduce conflicts in
the international community.[58]

It is conceded that under existing law coastal states possess sovereign rights to marine mineral resources on the bed of the territorial
sea and of the continental shelf adjacent to their land territory. However, under the definition of the continental shelf areas are included
which are adjacent to the coast in instances where the waters make
possible the exploitation of mineral resources. Progress in technology
will permit exploitation at increasing depths. A coastal state could
assert claim to a shelf of indeterminate width, in waters of undesig-
nated depths; the one requirement is that the area shall be "adjacent
to the coast." The continental shelf lacks a definitive seaward limit.[59]

Moreover, the law of the sea beyond the shelf is conjectural. The present law serves to encourage the claiming of wide continental shelves by coastal states, with distorting effects upon rights of other states. There is need for a redefinition of the continental shelf.

Regardless of what the ultimate redefinition of the continental shelf may be, exploitation of mineral resources in the deep sea beyond the shelf is already within technological competence. Therefore the predominant juridical issue that is emerging concerns the entity or body entitled to regulate the right of exploitation of these resources. Questions may relate to the basis of exploitative rights and the limitations attached thereto. In general terms, the issue might well be between interested states having certain compatible points of agreement and control by the international community. Consensus may be lacking as to whether new juridical concepts or political mechanisms of any type may appropriately be advocated at present or when there should be enactment of particular law pertaining to the deep sea. Should an entity or body be established for exploitation of resources of deep oceanic areas?[60]

In forthcoming deliberations regarding the legal regime that should control the deep seas exploitation there will doubtless be a reiteration of *res nullius* and *res communis*. Governments will assert positions concerning the vast source of natural resources—the deep seas. Already governments have proposed regimes for the administration of such resources, yet few, if any, governments will adopt uncontrolled *res nullius* for the advantaged nations and the international hazard of injurious competitive practices or conflicting uses.

Obviously, divergence of view has been expressed in proposals for new legal safeguards concerning the seas' resources and the need for immediacy of legal action.

VARIOUS ALTERNATIVE REGIMES FOR MARINE RESOURCES UNDERLYING
THE HIGH SEAS

Scope of Proposals

Various international regimes and new legal safeguards have been proposed for the harvesting and distribution of the sea's resources. In an international regime nation-states might relinquish substantial autonomy and voluntarily accept the jurisdiction of an international body. In such a case, extraction of the sea's resources would be accomplished by the body. Another basic plan for an international regime would permit state exploitation upon authorization from the international body; extractions would be controlled and regulated by the body. The term *international* would refer to a comprehensive intergovernmental institution such as the United Nations and its specialized agencies. Attention should also be given to the possibility of reserving areas of the deep sea to solutions by regional organizations. Such an arrangement could be effected by general treaty, by customary practices, or by consensus in the United Nations. Even under a system of national arrangements regional organizations might still negotiate with a nation or nations. Also, an international regime might negotiate with regional organizations.[61] Another proposal has advocated an international system for the issuance of licenses for exploitation of marine resources. The authorized body would have competence to issue licenses or permits to governments or to their nationals by procedures based on request, by competitive bidding, or by a principle of geographic distribution. Such systems would require the promulgation of regulations by the authorized body concerning competence for exploitation and intention to harvest; the dimension of an area to be granted to individual applicants; proximity of leases; forfeiture in instances of failure in exploitation; tenure of leases; and royalty charges. The net income would be diverted to specific international purposes. Such a regime, it has been asserted, would accept national exploitation of the seabed; there would be international regulation of exploitation; and the principle of *res communis* would be accommodated. Participants would presumably derive a profit, and the international community would derive benefits through the international fund. Exploitation would be accelerated, development would be orderly, and harsh competitive practices would be avoided. Entrepreneurial investors would be protected against nationalization or disproportionate royalties or taxes, as well as immunized against changing political regimes (as is illustrated in situations which have arisen in the Middle East or in Nigeria). This plan, it has been further affirmed, would result in the minimizing of hazards inherent in extensions of national sovereignty and in possible intrusion upon other traditional uses; it would encourage international cooperation.[62] Arguments opposing such a plan would involve basic interference with national sovereignty;

the body should be subject to "checks and balances" as insurance against usurpation and abusive practices. A bureaucracy would be necessary, including adjudicative authority. Major policy decisions, speculative information which might involve major consequences for the supply of resources for international distribution, and world markets are major considerations. For example, a decision might involve the differentiation between simultaneous applications for the production of petroleum or for the mining for gold. Control of production would be essential to avoid depleting effects on the market or future supplies; mining privileges might be denied because of an international disagreement. These varied decisions are capable of affecting national interests of applicants and of all countries, with repercussions of political controversy. The responsibility of such a body would be momentous. Also, arguments abound opposing a system of international license or asserting that a new regime would constitute a hazard to the traditional freedom of the sea for many uses.[63] Certain objections might be forestalled by the limitation of the purposes, functions, and authority of the international entity. Licenses might be restricted to applicant states; the state government might exploit the area or enter into a contractual agreement with individual entrepreneurs as a sublicensee. Respective states in the international agreement might determine the terms and conditions of licenses, thus precluding the exercise of large discretionary powers by the international authority. Through a process of meticulous description and circumscribed functions, the body might be restricted to a ministerial capacity. This in effect would be tantamount to a registry system with certain police and adjudicatory authority. A change in policies may entail compromises to attain general acceptability, and agreement would be affected by revenue provisions, sums involved, purposes of distribution, and the method of decisions and expenditures.[64]

International operation for the exploitation of natural resources would debar states and private companies from participation; such a plan would grant a monopoly to an international entity, corporation, or consortium (intergovernmental, private, or combined). The designated entity would have contractual powers for procuring technically competent personnel and equipment. There would be predetermination of all national interests; the purchase of shares in fixed ratios would be permissible. Alternately, the entity, corporation, or consortium might be equally owned by all nations with proportionate participation in derived profits.[65]

Ultimately, there will be a preference between an international system of licensing operated by an international entity with restricted powers and a national regime under which an international organization would operate a registry, monitor, settle disputes, and collect revenues. In one system, the state has freedom of choice as to where and when it will begin the exploitation, with observance of rules and regulations of registration and payment of designated fees. The other system would prohibit operation by a state until the granting of approval by the international authority.[66]

Acceptability of These Proposals

In a consideration of alternate regimes for the administration of deep sea mineral resources it is necessary to ascertain the viability of the regime under examination and whether it would promote the "economically efficient, peaceful, and orderly exploitation of the minerals of the sea floor."[67]

Three criteria will determine the success of the regime: economically efficient operations, acceptability to a sufficient number of nations, and feasibility. The primary requisite for an economically efficient enterprise is the guarantee of exclusive rights of exploration and exploitation for a sufficient area of specified duration. Efficient managerial programs for the minerals of the deep sea may necessitate revenue to the public, whether the public be of the flag nation or of the community of nations.[68]

Relative to acceptability, the regime will be judged, accepted or rejected, according to views of nations having decisive influence as to whether the regimes encompass an equitable distribution of economic net gains to participant nations.

The third criterion of the legal regime is that of feasibility. Such a regime might well necessitate the devolopment of new institutions for administrative purposes, enforcement, and adjudication.[69]

General alternatives to be considered in efforts to devise an acceptable regime to control the minerals of the deep ocean floor may be categorized as international, regional and national, unilateral, or coastal state.

It is the contention of opponents to an international regime that such a regime is unnecessary because after controversies emerge, international law can respond through the injection of essential rules. However, the issue of the possible division of the treasure of the seas would be beyond the probability of immediate decision. It has been suggested that reliance on a satisfactory evolution of international law is uncertain and that plans should be formulated for future contingencies.[70]

As to terms of probable acceptability to states of various alternative legal procedures or regimes pertaining to mining deep-sea mineral resources, it may be stated that:

1. Some states are in accord with provisions set forth in the Geneva Convention on the Continental Shelf and sanction a broad interpretation of the exploitability clause in Article 1.[71]

2. Other states contend that the Geneva Convention fails in declaratory terms of international customary law and that freedom may be exercised in opposition to any plan or program which may be opposed to national interests and which may be interpreted as contradictory to international customary law.[72]

3. Certain states possessing limited geographical shelves are expected to oppose any depth criterion for the seaward limit of the continental shelf advanced thus far. The Latin American states particularly, for asserted reasons of exclusive national claims, frequently fail to clarify their interest in the natural resources of the seabed and subsoil and their concern in maximizing national exclusive fishery areas.[73]

4. Other states less fortunate in geographical placement than the North Sea states will be cognizant of boundary divisions of the North Sea continental shelf among adjacent states, including areas at an approximate distance of 170 miles from the nearest coast.[74]

5. Thus far only developed states possess financial and technological competence for the exploitation of submarine resources; however, present international attitudes, supported *inter alia* by the United Nations Development Program, indicate hostility toward further enrichment of developed states and emphasize assistance to lesser developed states to enable them to participate in an equitable apportionment of submarine resources by the execution of preinvestment surveys and the provision of technical and monetary assistance.[75]

6. Attitudes of petroleum and mineral companies will necessarily be considered, since they will have the responsibility of exploitative

technological competence and the advance capital investment of vast sums.[76]

It may be assumed that commercial enterprises in the western states will be commissioned to explore and exploit the known resources of the deep seas, regardless of the nature of the ultimate international legal regime. Any proposed international regime would require authority to protect the investors in submarine activities against undue financial risks. Entrepreneurs would essentially require security against hazards emerging from an unstable legal regime, such as unresolved claims to an exaggerated continental shelf by a state not a participant in a deep-sea "conventional arrangement,"[77] as well as against unforeseeable policies and processes of an international entity which might be created for regulation of deep-sea exploitation. Investors would, moreover, require protective measures against expropriation or other injurious practices of the concessionary state and against hostilities in the area.[78]

Review of Specific Proposals

At present, there is increased interest in the manifold problems of exploration and exploitation for peaceful purposes of the resources on the seabed and its subsoil, extending beyond the boundaries of national jurisdiction, together with a conviction expressed by some that such exploitation should be for the benefit of all mankind, with particular recognition of the needs of lesser developed nations.[79]

Indicative of the complexity and dissimilarity of issues expressed by certain nation-states of the world community concerning the exploitation and equitable distribution of mineral resources of the seabed and subsoil beyond national jurisdiction are the various legal procedures and regimes which have been promulgated. Four approaches seem dominant: (1) an international regime, under the aegis of the United Nations or one of its specialized agencies; (2) an international-regional regime; (3) a regional regime; and (4) national control over near shore ocean areas.

International Regime

Political interest in the issues involved in the exploitation of oceanic mineral resources is indicated by United Nations General Assembly resolutions by governmental and nongovernmental organizations as well as by reports and voluminous publications.[80]

Certain proposals include advocacy of international mechanisms or agencies with realistic control and regulatory powers for the mineral resources of the deep oceans. Such regulation would include execution and enforcement of agreements eventually made with respect to ownership and distribution of the inanimate resources of the sea.[81]

Maltese Proposal

International control and regulation of deep-sea resources was advocated by the diminutive island of Malta through Permanent Representative of Malta to the United Nations Dr. Arvid Pardo, at the twenty-second session of the General Assembly, on August 18, 1967. The Maltese government submitted the issue of the exclusive reservation for peaceful objectives of the seabed and the ocean floor, and the subsoil thereof, underlying the high seas beyond the areas of national jurisdiction and the utilization of their resources for the benefit of mankind:

1. the preservation of the international character of the sea-bed . . . . beyond the limits of present national jurisdiction, not as a *res omnium communis*, usable for any convenient purpose and the resources of which are indiscriminately and competitively exploitable, but through the acceptance by the international community that these vast areas of our planet have a special status as a common heritage of mankind and, as such, should be reserved exclusively for peaceful purposes and administered by an international agency in the name and for the benefit of all peoples and of present and future generations.[82]

Ambassador Pardo, in offering the resolution in the General Assembly, called for a multi-nation treaty which would (1) grant the United Nations title to the seabed beyond present national jurisdiction, (2) establish an international agency for the administration of marine resources, (3) provide for the allocation of revenues from those resources "primarily to promote the development of poor countries," and (4) reserve the ocean floor "exclusively for peaceful purposes in perpetuity," thus prohibiting weaponry on the ocean floor.[83]

Dr. Pardo reiterated that the ad hoc committee created in December, 1967, by the General Assembly

to study the elaboration of the legal principles and norms which would promote international cooperation in the exploration and use of the sea-bed and ocean floor and the subsoil thereof, beyond the limits of national jurisdiction and to insure the exploitation of their resources for the benefit of mankind and other requirements . . . [and to review] studies . . . in the field of exploration and research . . . aimed at intensifying international cooperation and . . . dissemination of scientific knowledge on the subject

was an international forum where the issue surrounding the seabed beyond national jurisdiction may be presented to this committee or forum for analysis.

A deterrent to the establishment of an international regime for the administration of marine resources beyond national jurisdiction is the lack of international norms for the definition of limits of the continental shelf over which states possess sovereign rights for the purpose of exploration and resource exploitation.[84] A legal vacuum exists concerning mineral exploitation in the area, since no adequate legal framework has been established.

Pell Treaty Proposal

Another effort to establish an international regime for oceanic areas beyond national jurisdiction was made in 1968 by U.S. Senator Claiborne Pell in his "Treaty on Principles Governing the Activities of States in the Exploration and Exploitation of Ocean Space."

The predominant features of the Pell Treaty are:

1. It considers in detail the applicability of outer-space law to ocean space. This includes freedom of exploration, cooperation, mutual assistance, mutual inspection, the status of vessels and installations, prohibition of weapons of mass destruction, relations to the United Nations, and ratification procedures.

2. It accords to international nongovernmental organizations a status almost commensurate with that of nations.

The Pell Treaty advocates the issuance of licenses for exploration and exploitation to either states or nongovernmental international organizations. There is a provision that "when such activities are carried out by an international organization, a license may be issued to such organization as if it were a state."

The licensing agency would be empowered to issue licenses to member states for the peaceful and orderly exploration and exploitation of the natural resources of the seabed and subsoil of submarine areas of the ocean space, and (1) to issue such licenses to international organizations and corporations; (2) to decide between two or more contending parties in the issuance of licenses; (3) to fix the size and dimension of the area under terms of the license; (4) to fix the period of the validity of the license; (5) to fix the payment of a fee or royalty; (6) to make such reasonable terms as it judges essential for the implementation of the treaty; (7) to stipulate terms for the most competent recovery of the resources consistent with conservation practices and with the avoidance of dissipating the natural resources of the seabed and subsoil of ocean space, and to circularize pertinent data obtained from licensees with respect to their operations in ocean space; (8) to inspect all stations, installations, equipment, sea vehicles, machines, and capsules on the seabed or in the subsoil of ocean space; (9) to command the licensee with respect to the suspension, modification, or prohibition of operations or experiments if such activities might cause potentially injurious obstruction to the peaceful exploration and exploitation of ocean space; (10) to levy fines and to revoke licenses for violation of the provisions of the treaty; (11) to provide regulative terms with regard to pollution and the disposal of radioactive waste elements in ocean space; to serve as arbiters and make awards; and (12) to establish an Ocean Guard under the aegis of the U.N. Security Council.[85]

These comprehensive powers awarded to the licensing agency contain no description of the character or constitution of the agency. The cogent inquiry has been made: Who is to exercise these encompassing powers? Would such power be conferred upon a super-bureaucracy? Responsible to whom? By whom would the agency be controlled? To whom would the agency be responsible? The principal deficiency of the Pell Treaty is apparently its failure to identify the entity or agency which would administer the immense program for regulating oceanic activities. A second deficiency in this treaty is that under its provisions the licensing agency exercises the powerful triple function of legislative, executive, and judicial powers. (These powers are set forth in Articles 21 and 22.) If decisions remain unresolved beyond a reasonable period of time, they are submitted to a panel of members appointed by the International Court of Justice. Subsequently they are submitted to the members of the court, although there is a provision that nongovernmental international organizations shall act independently, and these organizations are not recognized before the International Court.[86]

The further provision in the treaty for supervisory responsibility by the U.N. Security Council over the proposed Ocean Guard would appear to be unacceptable to certain member states. The agency is to be designated by the United Nations, with sanction of the Security Council in conformity with terms of paragraph 3 of Article 27 of the Charter of the United Nations. The Ocean Guard would be under the aegis of the licensing agency but responsible to the Security Council, despite the Council's record of difficulties concerning peacekeeping forces and activities.[87]

The dilemma of the definition of the ocean floor also appears in the Pell Treaty. The treaty proposals would limit the continental shelf—subject to the jurisdiction of the littoral state—to a depth of six hundred meters, thus abrogating the open-endedness of the Geneva Convention of 1958. Such a depth limitation would appear to be unjustifiable geologically and politically, since the result would be a deprivation in certain instances in which there is a steep descending coastline. Thus the area might be less than twelve miles, while in other instances it would extend for hundreds of miles.[88]

The Pell Treaty follows the general proposals set forth in the treaty on Principles Governing the Use of Outer Space, Including the Moon and Other Celestial Bodies, and the Antarctic Treaty. Fundamentally the draft treaty, with its preamble and nine parts, prohibits the extension of national sovereign rights into ocean space. Moreover, exploration and exploitation of the seabed and subsoil of the submarine areas in such space may be exercised only upon authorization by a licensing agency and the issuance of licenses subject to stated criteria. The licenses are granted for not more than a fifty-year period, with an option of renewal. Cancellation of licenses is provided for noncompliance with terms.[89]

Danzig Proposed Treaty

Another proposed treaty urging the internationalization of activities concerned with the exploration and use of the resources of the deep seas and ocean floor is also structured upon the Treaty on Outer Space. This document, with its appended comments, was the proposal of the United Nations Committee of the World Peace through Law Center and is entitled "Proposed Treaty Governing the Exploration and Use of the Ocean Bed." Its author, Aaron L. Danzig, is chairman of the drafting committee of this organization.[90]

The Danzig Treaty contains a Prefatory Note and Comment proposing the establishment of an Ocean Agency to be entrusted with exclusive accountability for the allocation of exploitation rights to the ocean bed. This would be a specialized agency of the United Nations. However, in the text there is no indication of the composition of such supervisory agency. Provisions include:

1. A tribunal is proposed, which would be affiliated with the agency yet whose membership and decision-making would be independent of it to adjudicate disputes originating in the responsibilities of the agency.

2. The ocean bed is defined to limit the continental shelf to approximate the average geological measurement of all continental shelves (200-meter depth or 50 miles beyond shore, whichever is greater, adding a horizontal dimension to the vertical dimension of the continental shelf).

3. It is contemplated that the shelf will be legally widened for countries having limited or no geological shelves. However, limitation of the shelf would be less than claims set forth by certain littoral states.

4. The Ocean Agency would have structural aspects similar to the original conception of the Special Fund of the United Nations. The functions of the agency would be fundamentally economic; the distribution of licenses would be made in compliance with non-arbitrary guidelines.

5. The agency would promote and protect scientific research and development. It is assumed that the personnel of the agency would include industrialists, economists, and scientists. Since the objectives of the agency are primarily economic and scientific, its controlling body would presumably be appointed or elected by the Economic and Social Council.

6. The treaty is confined basically to a delineation of the jurisdiction of the agency over the resources of the ocean bed, yet the interdependence of ocean bed and ocean waters is recognized, with ineluctable legal significance.

7. The agency is vested with specifically restricted power to enlarge its scope, should there arise a necessity for such action, to the extent of granting licenses relative to mineral and other inanimate resources which are contained in ocean waters and issuing regulations appertaining thereto.

8. There is provision in the treaty for the reservation of the ocean bed for peaceful objectives only, with permission for justifiable defense activities within the purview of inspection requisites of the treaty.

9. No portion of the ocean bed or of any of its resources is to be subject to national or individual appropriation or exclusive utilization by claim of sovereignty, use, occupation, or other means. The terms are designed to reserve to the agency the exclusive right to issue licenses for explorative or exploitation purposes. Article III contains more stringent restrictions on national sovereignty than those appearing in Article II of the Treaty on Outer Space, which provides: "Outer Space, including the Moon and other celestial bodies, is not subject to national appropriation by claim of sovereignty, by means of use or occupation, or any other means."[91] With certain prohibitions concerning military uses, states may utilize portions of celestial bodies in any manner, with the exception of interference with exploratory activities of other nations. Colonization in preselected areas is permitted; resources of celestial bodies may be used and removed for the states' own benefit; and moreover, states may establish laws and regulations applicable to their nationals.[92]

Subsequent articles of the Danzig Treaty provide that states parties to the treaty shall be governed in conformity with international law, including the Charter of the United Nations:

1. The states shall be prohibited from emplacement of weaponry of mass destructive capability on the ocean bed. The ocean bed shall be used exclusively for peaceful purposes.

2. The states shall be internationally responsible for national activities on the ocean bed.

3. The terms of license would compel the licensee to consent to submit to tribunal jurisdiction all disputes emanating from activities resulting from such licenses.

4. The states shall retain jurisdiction and control over objects placed in or on the ocean floor or by their nationals or juridical persons.[93]

5. Activities shall be subject to observation by the Ocean Agency.

Article XIII states in part that: There is established an Ocean Agency. Said agency shall be brought into relationship with the United Nations by appropriate agreement.[94]

The states parties to the treaty grant to the said agency exclusive
authority to administer:

exclusive and non-exclusive exploration and exploitation rights pertaining to the
ocean bed, and to fix charges thereof to be paid to said Agency. . . . [the]
Treaty . . . shall not, . . . interfere with any rights of States Parties to this Treaty
derived from the Convention on the Territorial Sea and the Contiguous zone, . . .
and other Conventions adopted by the United Nations Conference on the Law of
the Sea April 29, 1958. . . . The income derived by the Agency, from the grant
of such exploration and exploitation rights shall be utilized to defray the expenses
of the Agency, any excess to accrue and be paid to the United Nations. . . . In
its discretion, if it shall determine that the purposes and objectives of this Treaty
shall require the same, the Agency may enlarge its jurisdiction to cover all or any
part of the non-living resources of the ocean waters beyond the territorial sea, in
which event the rights, powers and privileges ascribed to the Agency under this
Article XIII shall pertain to such resources, additionally.

The agency is empowered to exercise independent exploration and
exploitation rights, but only with regard to those resources for which
"governmental or non-governmental exploration or exploitation by
licensing arrangements are not readily available."[95]

Funds receivable from licensing fees, after payment of agency expenses, are allocated for the purposes specified in subparagraphs a
and b of Article 55 of the United Nations Charter. Discretionary
power is granted to the General Assembly to use up to 20 percent of
such funds for any other purpose included in the United Nations
Charter. The paramount purpose for which the funds are expected to
be used is the improvement of the economic, social, and cultural status
of mankind as a whole.

The licensing schedule envisaged for the agency requires an
equilibrium regarding two significant purposes: (a) economical and
efficient exploitation of resources of the seabed, and (b) encouragement to the developing states and their nationals to participate in
such exploitation.

The treaty seeks the accomplishment of these purposes by the
establishment of a nonarbitrary guideline for the issuance of licensing
based upon the "highest bidder approach," with regard to the competency and reliability of the bidding entity, with due care to avoid
monopolization of such economic enterprises. It also provides for
technical assistance to developing countries and their nationals under
subparagraph (a) of Article XIII. In addition, the article grants discretion to the agency to disregard the "highest bidder" criterion if the

granting of a license will assist a developing state or its nationals to improve its or their technological capability to explore or exploit the resources of the seabed.[96]

Neither the Pell Treaty nor the Danzig Treaty designates in its text the composition of the personnel of the proposed agency. The Danzig Treaty's provision for the creation of an Ocean Tribunal is a logical addition to terms of the treaty beyond the provisions found in the Pell Treaty. The Danzig proposal for an agency emanating from the U.N. Social and Economic Council fails to provide for methods of coordination and cooperation with the many existing organs and entities of the United Nations currently engaged in the area of ocean-ography and related topics. Assuming that the agency, appointed or elected by the Economic and Social Council, would necessarily be numerically small, many nations would lack representation in it. But if membership is not to be open to all nations, the problem arises as to whether the agency would gain acceptance by unrepresented nations. The Danzig Treaty fails to mention the General Assembly as a body to assist these nations, as is usually stipulated by statutes of specialized agencies. It might be asked whether there is an assumption that the governing agency should be responsible to the General Assembly of the United Nations. This would appear to be the implication, since the General Assembly regulates the disposition or allocation of reve-nues. However, the General Assembly, with its system of one-nation-one-vote, would probably lack adequacy for the responsibility. It may be contended that it is problematical that there will be excess revenue requiring administration by the U.N. General Assembly or any other entity, for forthcoming decades. However, in considering appropriate organizations for such an assignment, and in the eventuality that Ambassador Pardo's estimate of an annual six-billion-dollar revenue materialized, it would be essential to establish legal and constitutional norms with competency for equitable distributive powers.[97] The com-petency of the agency would necessarily presuppose recognition and acceptance by business, by industry, and by consumers who are factu-ally the peoples of the world community, in both developed and emerging nations, coastal and noncoastal nations, free-enterprise and socialist nations. This comprehensive collaboration would doubtless pose difficulties of considerable magnitude.[98]

It seems conjectural that an Ocean Assembly representative of all

nations on the foundation proposed by the Danzig Treaty would be
an improvement on the existing U.N. one-nation-one-vote system.[99]

Elizabeth Mann Borgese has stated:

> The simple fact is that no system of representation in the traditional political
> sense . . . is applicable to a world of some hundred and thirty nations with a
> proliferation of mini-nations and a reality of economic power in no way corres-
> ponding to the political reality. . . . We have come to the point where a . . .
> transition must be made—from representational democracy to participating de-
> mocracy. This need manifests itself dramatically in the international commu-
> nity. . . . New paths have to be set out: this is the problem. Could there be
> a more auspicious occasion than this one of Man's penetration of No Man's
> Land?[100]

Christy Proposal

Another proposal more general in nature has been made by Francis
Christy, Jr., an authority on ocean regime, who suggests that the
United Nations be authorized to establish a United Nations Authority
which will have exclusive jurisdiction over the resources on or beneath
the ocean floor. This authority would be given the power to convey
and protect the exclusive rights of entrepreneurs. The authority must
be empowered to tax or exact rental or royalty fees for the utilization
of the resources and to use or distribute such revenues in an appropriate manner. Certain adequate boundaries for the jurisdiction of the
authorities must be established which would also be necessary under
a flag nation regime.[101]

The operation of an international regime would enable the individual entrepreneur from any nation to bid for the exclusive right
to explore and exploit a given area for a designated resource. The
bid would indicate terms of royalty payment and agreement to pay
a certain fixed percentage of the gross revenue for the enterprise. A
bid might be on a percentage basis of net revenue, or payable as a
cash bonus on an installment basis. Exclusive claims to massive regions
of the sea might be forestalled by requirement of exploitation within
a specified period for development. An inspection plan would prevent
possible abuses of the lease rights and protect the marine environment. Such requirements are similar to requirements for exploitation
on the U.S. continental shelf.[102]

Christy admits the difficulty of determining a boundary between
the interests of the coastal state and those of the community of nations;
however, he is of the opinion that his suggested international regime

might facilitate the decision. He suggests that a higher percentage of royalty payment might be allocated to the coastal state for exploitation nearer to shore and the greater distance from shore would result in a larger percentage to the authority. This system would provide operation under uniform rules throughout the world ocean, and there would be diminishment of accelerated royalty rates and uncertainties related to expropriation.[103] In the opinion of Christy, such an international authority for the resources of the ocean floor is analogous to the administration and control of the petroleum resources of the U.S. continental shelf. The continental shelf resources are regarded as part of the public domain, and exploiters are granted exclusive lease rights. These rights are insured and an orderly process of exploitation is guaranteed by the federal government as administrator. The revenues derived from these cash bonuses and royalty fees are allocated for the benefit of the citizenry.[104]

Combination of International-Regional Regime

A second approach to the establishment of an acceptable and feasible regime for the administration of marine resources might be a system combining international and regional processes. Under such an association states would have greater latitude than under a delegated inflexible control by an international entity, the United Nations or one of its specialized agencies. States would act in a supervisory capacity to insure reasonable development of the resources. The Regional recording Agency would have, however, a central United Nations Index. When two states in the same region make area claims in that region, a regional organization might be formulated by a bilateral treaty stipulating the boundaries of each claim. This treaty would be open to accession by other regional states. Meanwhile recognition might be made of the exclusive jurisdiction and control of the specific areas claimed by each state for survey purposes for a limited period to permit the initial phase of exploitation in a restricted zone. Other claims might be recorded with the regional organization and evidence regarding the area and the nature of the claim would be considered. If the competence of the claimant to harvest the resources were established, registration would be automatically granted. The claimant would be given priority *inter partes* over other claims to the area. At the termination of the limited initial phase, the claim would receive recognition by the form of continued registration. Recognition of the claim would continue so long as evidence existed of competent recovery of the marine resources.[105]

In such a regime, some organ, agency, entity, or institution or body would necessarily be entrusted with competence to ascertain *inter alia* the capacity of the claimant to develop or exploit the mineral resources of hydrospace beyond national jurisdiction. Evidence of efficient and judicious recovery would be required. One possible method of acquiring such evidence might be to empower the registrar to make initial decisions in conformity with a code of recognized mining practices containing provision for appeal from these decisions to an international arbitral tribunal aided by expert assessors. This method might encourage an increase in the nucleus of states adhering to the treaty, especially under the tutelage of leading powers.[106]

Irrespective of whether a new juridical regime is established through the initiative of the United Nations or through other agreements, contentions may be expected as to whether the regime should be a regional, national, or international entity.

International regimes provide for significant powers and control by international organizations or entities and at least certain revenue available for international objectives. However, the various classifications are not mutually exclusive and are subject to variance in category. Factors may be transposed from one regime to the other, thereby creating an amalgamated or blended system of international-regional regimes.[107]

Regional or Coastal States Regime

In conjunction with considerations regarding national, international, or blended systems for the allocation of rights for amicable exploration and exploitation of mineral resources of the marine environment, regional or coastal state arrangements or agreements should be mentioned.

In general, if regional agreements were consummated, registration procedures might be inaugurated together with allocation of powers. Also there might be created a system for arbitration and adjudication in conflictive situations. Following adoption of preliminary procedures, regional agreements might eventually evolve into an amalgamated system under a specialized agency of the United Nations. During the transformational phase of this amalgamative effort, certain states might well decline to participate in regional treaty arrangements. Such disputes would then necessarily be resolved in conformity with international customary law. The process of establishing new rules of international customary law from the proposed treaty agreements may result in binding effect upon both participating and nonparticipating states.[108]

The significance of the adoption of an acceptable regime for undersea resources is intensified by the fact that of the 135 nations of the world community, 109 are littoral states and only 26 are landlocked. Of the 109 nations, approximately 40 have enacted legislation concerning minerals in the continental shelf. Also, of the 109 coastal states, approximately 36 have acceded to the 1958 Geneva Convention on the Continental Shelf. Relative to deep-sea areas extending seaward beyond the continental shelf, debate ensues among nations and individual international authorities with respect to the system of laws or regime which would be acceptable to the majority of littoral states.[109]

International agreements with regard to undersea boundaries have been made in three particular areas—the Gulf of Paria, the Persian Gulf, and the North Sea. As the last of these is the most important, discussion will be confined to that regime.

North Sea

Of these areas, only the North Sea is superjacent to a land area which in geological terms may be categorized as a continental shelf. The North Sea has had extensive offshore exploration and exploitation. The undersea boundaries will probably be fixed by the majority of participating coastal states in accord with principles of the Convention on the Continental Shelf, in view of the fact that the North Sea overlies a continental shelf. Five of the seven nations adjacent to the North Sea—the United Kingdom, Denmark, the Netherlands, Germany, and France—are signatories of the Geneva Convention.[110]

Apparently only two countries, the United Kingdom and Norway, have entered into formal agreement on their common boundary underlying the North Sea. However, Germany has reached an agreement with the Netherlands on a portion of their boundary. Nations which have yet to reach formal agreement are commendably following the

median lines in determining boundary solutions.[111] The United Kingdom–Norway agreement is in general conformity with the terms of
Article 6, inasmuch as the common boundary between the two nations
is a line "every point of which is equidistant from the nearest point
of the baselines from which the territorial sea of each country is
measured."[112]

The United Kingdom could have asserted valid sovereign rights
over the entire North Sea's seabed and subsoil

lying above a depth of two hundred meters from the surface of the sea and which
lies to the north of a parallel of latitude subtending westerly from the most south-
erly point on the south bank of the Norwegian Trench lying at a depth of 200
meters, and also to a slightly smaller area.[113]

The employment of either of the alternative methods of measurement based upon the 200 meters of depth criterion would, however,
have resulted in the exclusion of Norway. Therefore, the British
proclamations recognized a questionable Norwegian claim at least
"as far west as a median line between the two states." This acknow-
ledgment of a possible Norwegian claim indicated that British recognition of the claim was predicated upon the decision to exploit the
area immediately and to avoid the exploitation delay involved in a
litigable dispute.

In the general agreement between the United Kingdom and Norway, the government of the United Kingdom unilaterally set forth
a claim "only out to a line some miles *west* of a true median between
the Norwegian and British coasts."[114] This would indicate that terms
of "exploitability" and "continuity" were subordinated to achieve a
compromise, taking into consideration proximity on the same shelf
and also the observance of comity and equity standards between
nations. These considerations serve as guidelines for amicable solutions
of the question of national boundary limits. Article 6 of the 1958
Geneva Convention on the Continental Shelf provides:

1. Where the same continental shelf is adjacent to the territories of two or more
   states whose coasts are opposite each other, the boundary of the continental
   shelf appertaining to such state shall be determined by agreement between
   them. In the absence of agreement, and unless another boundary line is justified by special circumstances the boundary is the median line, every point of
   which is equidistant from the nearest points of the shoreline from which the
   breadth of the territorial sea of each state is measured.[115]

The waters of the North Sea are shallow, two hundred meters in depth. From a morphological viewpoint the Norwegian Trough, where depths are in excess of two hundred meters, is generally regarded as the limit of the edge of the shelf.[116] Geologically, the edge of the trough is a deep depression caused by glacial action, similar to evidences of glacial action existing on the mainland. The depression or trough is, therefore, regarded as an integral part of the shelf. The definition of the continental shelf in Article 1 relates to instances where submerged areas less than two hundred meters in depth situated in close proximity to the coastline are separated from that portion of the continental shelf contiguous to the coast by a channel deeper than two hundred meters. The significant inquiry is concerned with whether such a channel serves to delimit the sovereignty of the littoral state in the area. Norway successfully contended that this channel was only a depression in its continental shelf and claimed full sovereignty under the principle of equidistance. This claim has apparently been accepted by all adjacent countries.[117]

On a regional basis, certain North Sea coastal states have authorized petroleum and gas exploration in the North Sea, an area of some 222,000 square miles between the British Isles and the northwest coast of the European continent, and overlying the European continental shelf. The littoral states within the area are the United Kingdom, Norway, Denmark, the Federal Republic of Germany, the Netherlands, Belgium, and France.

For generations preceding the discovery of petroleum and gas deposits in the area, the North Sea was indispensable for fishing and commercial activities essential to the nationals of the coastal states. Because of its unique combination of natural elements, including water temperature, source of food, and nature of the seabed, it had been recognized as one of the bountiful fishing areas of the world.[118]

Sea traffic is another major use of the North Sea. Existing economic conditions have increased maritime activities in the area. Greater complications have arisen with the extension of offshore petroleum and gas exploitation and the demands of the European economy for new and convenient sources of energy.

The quest for energy in Western Europe was directed to the North Sea after the discovery of the large natural gas field in Groningen in 1959. On both the coastal and offshore areas of the North Sea there were indications of promising yields of petroleum and gas. Initial explorative activities in the North Sea have been off the coasts of the United Kingdom, Norway, Denmark, West Germany, and the Netherlands.[119]

The United Kingdom, with the largest North Sea shelf area, began in 1964 the establishment of a comprehensive legal system applicable to offshore exploration and exploitation operations. On May 11, 1964, it became the twenty-second state to ratify the Convention on the Continental Shelf. The British Continental Shelf Act 1964, enacted on April 15, 1964, was drawn in concurrence with provisions of the convention. In accordance with its regulations, the British government divided the designated area into blocks of approximately 250 square kilometers each and made bids available. In initial awards in September, 1964, twenty-two companies and groups received production offshore licenses for some 346 blocks.[120]

In late 1964 only one of seven North Sea states, the United Kingdom, was a party to the Convention on the Territorial Sea. Only two, Denmark and the United Kingdom, were parties to the Convention on the Continental Shelf. Activities in the North Sea are generally controlled by principles of general international law and certain agreements among the coastal states, on a reciprocal basis in conformity with terms of the Geneva Conventions.[121]

All of the North Sea states except Norway maintain their advocacy of a three-mile limit for the extent of the territorial sea. Norway's four-mile limit and its method of straight baselines are no longer controversial topics. Apparently, a similar consensus prevails with regard to the continental shelf. The five North Sea states possessing potentially large reserves in submarine resources recognize the exclusive appurtenance of the resources to the littoral state. The division of such resources by equidistant boundary lines seems to be acceptable to the North Sea coastal states, in the absence of contrary agreements. It is possible that Germany may attempt readjustment by certain agreements.[122]

Consensus on the part of participating states seems to point to amicable solutions concerning the delimitation and control of offshore areas. Two general types of problems may exist: (1) those related to the exploitation of submarine resources in the North Sea and the delimitation of the various national areas, together with competent recovery of such resources, problems which are mainly technical, which are soluble, and in which municipal legislation may be applicable and acceptable; and (2) possible conflicts among different uses of the same area in the marine environment.

General provisions of the Continental Shelf Convention set forth principles applicable to exploitation activities and other uses of the sea, and specify in Article 4 that the littoral state may not "impede the laying of submarine cables or pipelines on the shelf, subject to a right for taking reasonable means for the exploration and exploitation of the resources."

There is affirmance of the rule in Article 5(1) that such exploration and exploitation must not result in "any unjustifiable interference with navigation, fishing or the conservation of the living resources of the sea," or in any interference with "fundamental scientific research." Article 516 prohibits the construction of installations or zones which might result in interference in the use of recognized sea lanes which are deemed essential to international navigation.

The coastal states have the responsibility to make decisions for the region of their continental shelf relative to adjustments for the various uses of the sea. Conflictive uses of the sea within the respective coastal states may find solutions through municipal domestic political processes.[123] Installations may result in navigational hazards; the inadvertent spillage of oil and noxious substances may result in contamination of waters; and seismological survey procedures which include the detonation of dynamite charges beneath the waters may cause injury in fishery areas. There may be interference with navigation. The convention prohibits installations in essential international sea lanes. Inquiries may be concerned with whether recognized sea lanes are to be considered in terms of immutability or whether after one notice reasonable relocation might be permitted in order to accommodate exploitation by the coastal state, if resources were found beneath the original sea lane course. The width of the sea lane might be significant, since certain offshore operations are contingent upon the availability of definite areas. Sea lanes may be three miles wide for shipping interests, while in some instances drilling operations would suffer loss if submarine mineral deposits were existent beneath such a three-mile area. A two-mile limit for a sea lane might be sought for such activities by developers of offshore petroleum deposits. Also, Article 4 of the Shelf

Convention prohibits a coastal state from summarily removing a pre-existing cable or pipeline on its shelf to accommodate its exploitation of marine resources in the same area. The test, according to M. S. McDougal and W. T. Burke, is reasonable use when considered in regard to all relevant elements.[124]

The equitable resolution of questions of competitive uses will entail a consideration of the relative economic importance of the interests to each state, as well as the overall benefits or detriments of such usage to the states and region.

Richard Young expressed the conviction that precedents and analogies exist in fishery arrangements applicable to the North Sea to serve as a basis for further study and recommendations concerning offshore claims and problems in that area. He is of the opinion that the North Sea states may easily agree on arbitral and judicial methods of settlement of such issues as may arise which are outside the scope of other means of adjudication. The problems are regional in nature and are often technical; therefore a special tribunal or system of tribunals might be acceptable to coastal states in the region of the North Sea.[125]

The Goldie Regional Regime Proposal

The principles for a regional regime have been proposed by L.F.E. Goldie; the proposal includes a design to assure legal title to mineral resources appropriated from the seabed and subsoil and provides that the appropriation be governed by the municipal law of each signatory state. Under the terms of this regime there would be recognition in the courts of all pertinent municipal laws through processes of international agreement or treaty. Goldie forewarns that such a regime is diametrically opposed to the doctrine of occupation or "first come first served" policies. He further states that in his view the time has not yet arrived to bestow discretionary powers upon an international agency for granting territory to states, or the right to win and appropriate resources to individuals. He advocates policy goals to secure titles and limited access to a resource to avoid overcapitalization, overproduction, and congestion of production in specified zones. In order to circumvent conflicting claims, regional agencies with affiliation in the United Nations Secretariat might be created to arrange for *evidentiary* (notice) and *recording* functionary duties. Goldie makes commendable comments to the effect that the International Telecommunications Union (ITU) performs functions of a nature similar to his proposals; it is an agency of the United Nations and has had singular success for over a century, and for years before its affiliation with the United Nations and the Economic and Social Council.[126]

The Goldie Regional Regime proposal contains ten sections. There is for example, provision in broad terms for:

1. The recognition of a right inuring to signatory states to acquire, and have recorded, specialized zones of jurisdiction and control whereby they would be enabled to give legal title over resources appropriated from the sea-bed and subsoil to their citizens (whether individuals or corporations) under their own municipal laws. Such zones of special jurisdiction would, in addition to clothing physical appropriations with legal rights, enable the recording state, under whose jurisdiction the zone was recorded, to protect the enterprises working the areas within its competency from piracy, theft, violence, trespasses of all kinds . . . .

2. The establishment of international recording agencies, organized on regional bases, with a central index in the United Nations Secretariat. . . . These agencies would have power to issue instruments defining the recording state's zone of Special Jurisdiction. . . .

6. The authority of a state exercising the jurisdiction and control . . . should be limited to the working of the specific resource which had been initially recorded (or registered) with it. . . .

7. . . . the special jurisdiction would be limited as to time. . . .

8. . . . states sovereign rights over recorded zones of special jurisdiction should be limited as to areas. . . .

The conclusion was drawn that a treaty regime incorporating principles enumerated in the above mentioned articles would secure titles to appropriated resources . . . and by limiting access to any given commodity would tend to minimize overcapitalization and losses occasioned by "overproduction and congestion." Second, the regime offers an alternative to the exploitability test—"the need to secure titles to resources taken from beyond the shelf region." The proposed regime avoids the "indeterminacy" inherent in Article 1's exploitability test.[127]

National Regime

In general terms, national regimes connote substantive and autonomous powers for states and their nationals, subject to possible bilateral or multilateral agreements among the state parties with respect to cooperative measures for the avoidance of conflict and the adjustment of disputes.

National regimes would permit the exploitation of the resources of the sea by any nation on a "first come" basis.

Certain suggestions which have been made would regard the seas as "international lakes." By a new convention or by protocol there would be agreement by nations that exploitation would be restricted to coastal states alone. By interpretation, the continental shelf would be considered as extending seaward for an undetermined distance or to the line where one "extended shelf" meets the equidistant boundary of another nation. Boundaries would be established in conformity with principles enunciated by the 1958 Convention.[128]

The national exploitation of marine resources would be conducive to an orderly development; experienced nations would participate under similar procedures and subject to regulatory measures presently in effect on the continental shelf. Mining companies would operate according to their municipal law and would have protection through traditional means. Coastal states would be protected against foreign intrusions of installations adjacent to their shores. Occasions for possible international disputes would be minimized. There would be less likelihood of further exclusive claims to excessive extensions of territorial sovereignty. This plan would avoid undue competitiveness in exploitation and the special disadvantages of and objections to international control.

However, in the opinion of Louis Henkin such a regime could not be adopted since other nations would object to the economic advantage and exclusive control of the marine resources and the danger posed to the traditional freedom of the seas.[129] The legal structure or regime which should be adopted to govern the exploration and development of minerals underlying the high seas exceeding the scope of the Convention on the Continental Shelf has been the subject of international debate.

The view of a national regime would recognize the right of the discovering nation to appropriate submerged lands, a principle historically accepted with respect to the acquisition of dominion over landmasses. In this category, the law of the flag of the discovering nation determines the ownership of the discovery.[130] Under this system of laws, unilateral legislation would extend to the new property rights, with due cognizance of the law of the sea with regard to the overlying waters.

Northcutt Ely presents practical considerations in his view supporting a national regime for the administration of deep sea resources.

Large investments are essential for deep sea mineral exploration and even larger sums, on the order of hundreds of millions of dollars, for exploitation. Only the private sectors of the mineral interests of the world community have access to these vast sums. Presently undersea operations will be conducted directly or indirectly with government funds. The number of governments so engaged will probably be limited to less than one dozen nations when financial capacity, maritime experience, and technological competence are taken into consideration. Governments having the initiative and capacity for submarine mineral exploration and operations have many interests in the deep ocean, including military and defense mechanisms. Permission to engage in these activities has not been sought from the United Nations thus far, and it seems problematical that such permission will be sought for the present.[131]

Ely continued his support for a national regime by stating:

> Nor is there any particular reason for these countries to concede taxes and royalties to a non-sovereign administrative agency for the granting of a right which it only obtained power to grant because they elected to create such a device. The United Nations' primary function is that of a mediator, not a sovereign.[132]

He further stated that two or three decades may be required to transpose existing mineral laws into applicability to undersea operations, or to evolve new legal principles. He concluded: "Let the law on this subject evolve as case law, not as codes prefabricated in a vacuum."[133]

Registration of National Regimes with an International Body

In addition to the four alternative regimes for the administration of deep sea nonliving resources, a dual concept might be devised by registration of national claims, together with a code of national conduct in regard to the occupation and utilization of the area under claim. These concepts are analogous to existing municipal mining laws in various countries.[134] Such a system of national laws would require the recording in an international registry office, by the flag nation sponsoring the expedition of a statement of intention to occupy a specific area of predetermined size. Thereafter, an exclusive right of occupancy of the published area would accrue to the recording nation, secured for an ascertained period of time for the benefit of its licensees.

In the event of the recovery of minerals, their production would be controlled by the nation which registered the initial notice of intent.[135]

The Committee on Deep Sea Mineral Resources of the American Branch of the International Law Association in its Interim Report stated disagreement with certain contentions that the above-mentioned system would be conducive to "anarchy" or "chaos." This approach is not categorized as absence of law, since existing law recognizes competence by a state to establish limited rights of jurisdiction and control over resources of the seabed upon effective use of the area. However, the committee recognized the inadequacy of these principles for extended developmental tenures.[136]

The committee expressed itself as being against "any attempt at a solution through the creation of an international licensing mechanism . . . , in the foreseeable future. To create and define the powers of such a supranational authority would be an enterprise rivaling in magnitude the creation of the United Nations." It recommended that an international commission be created or responsibility be vested in an existing commission which would create an international agency with limited functions of (1) receiving, recording, and publishing notices by sovereign nations of intent to occupy and explore respective areas of the seabed exclusively for mineral production, notices of occupation and discovery, and regular notices of continued operation, and (2) resolving conflicts between notices recorded by two or more state occupants within the same area of exploitation.[137]

The encompassing question of a future regime of the oceans has generated international debate relative to deep-ocean mineral resources. Generally a proposal governing the seabed beyond the continental shelf originates from either a national or an international approach. A national viewpoint incorporates the assumption that the resources of the ocean floor are *res nullius* and consequently subject to national appropriation. In an international approach there is an assumption that the resources are *res communis*, which would preclude permanent national appropriation of the seabed in areas seaward from the continental shelf. This approach would bring about the internationalization of the seabed and its subsoil beyond the limits of national jurisdiction and the establishment of an international entity, presumably under the aegis of the United Nations.[138]

In December, 1968, the 23rd General Assembly adopted three

resolutions, the first of which created a Committee on the Peaceful Uses of the Seabed and the Ocean Floor beyond the Limits of National Jurisdiction, composed of forty-two states. This committee received instruction to study legal principles and norms to promote international cooperation on the exploration and use of the seabed and ocean floor beyond the limits of national jurisdiction. The second resolution dealt with problems of pollution and the third with support of the International Decade of Ocean Exploration.[139]

Concerning the administration of marine resources underlying the high seas, William T. Burke has expressed a cogent negative view, focusing attention on certain substantive and procedural recommendations contained in the proposal of the Commission to Study the Organization of Peace in its Nineteenth Report of March, 1969, for vesting title in the United Nations to marine mineral resources beyond the area of the continental shelf. Burke objects to the failure of the commission to present even "the slightest attempt to identify the need for haste . . . for urgent and immediate action." The report, he asserts, contains no "remote hint of the factors that call for precipitate measures." "If we are to concur in a recommendation that about two-thirds of the earth be allocated to a single international government authority," he declares, "more comprehensive study and reporting are required." He outlines relevant factors in appraising the commission's recommendations. In part they are: (1) the defects of a piecemeal approach to ocean use, attempting to resolve one or two specific problems in isolation from others; (2) generally, the nascent state of ocean sciences and technology; (3) specifically, the present lack of knowledge of the technology of ocean mining; and (4) the fact that the development of a national ocean program is still in its early stages.[140]

Myres S. McDougal has expressed disagreement with Senator Pell's view concerning a twelve-mile contiguous zone for fisheries, stating that he was not at all sure that it was in the interest of this country or in the common interest of mankind that this country should claim such a zone. He further commented that "it may take a hundred years for the law of the sea to recover from the last two international conferences which dealt with [the contiguous zone for fisheries]," and that he "would regard the immediate call of another conference as an unmitigated disaster." He continued that the very function of the law of the sea is to protect the peoples of the world community and to secure their common interests. The law should reject all claims relating to special interest.[141]

Richard Young has stated that a durable and satisfactory regime for deep-sea floor resources must be founded on knowledge of geographical facts, of technological competence, present and to be anticipated, and of political and economic realities. It is prudent "to make haste slowly." An appraisal and synthesis of these factors cannot be achieved in the present state of knowledge and competence; no infrastructure of information is available for decisions concerning national and international interests in the marine environment. However, during the 1966 and 1967 sessions of the General Assembly, important resolutions were adopted by the United Nations. In the 1966 resolution the secretary general was requested to examine present knowledge with regard to marine resources and, with assistance from a group of experts, to evaluate marine science and technology; also, he was asked to prepare proposals for increased international cooperation for activities in inner space, for submission to the Assembly during the 1968 session.[142]

A proposal presented by the island-nation Malta in 1967 to the First Committee of the General Assembly resulted in the creation of an Ad Hoc Committee to Study the Peaceful Uses of the Seabed and the Ocean Floor beyond the Limits of National Jurisdiction. The Maltese proposal called for a "declaration and treaty concerning the reservation exclusively for peaceful purposes of the seabed and ocean floor, underlying the seas beyond present national jurisdiction, and the use of their resources in the interests of mankind."[143]

As a progressive measure, it has been urged that support be given to the Intergovernmental Oceanographic Agency pending the probable creation of a World Oceanic Agency. Such an entity of experienced individuals would be comparable to the twenty-three international fishery bodies and commissions which have functioned for a period of some six decades and are currently engaged in fishery conservation measures.[144] This "body of experience and practice" has set up examples which it has been said would be more useful among nations in finding solutions for joint problems emerging from the harvesting of the minerals of the deep-sea bed "than any formulation" put forward by the Pell, Danzig, or other proposals.[145]

Other scholars have opposed one or more proposals for the reason of technical imperfections or because international organizations lack governmental or administrative competence to manage marine affairs directly. According to Robert L. Friedman, many governments have indicated that in their opinion normative international proposals constitute an attack upon the state system generally. He states that

the west coast Latin American states probably would not object if a seabed or ocean agency controlled the resources up to twelve miles off the coasts of the United States, Soviet Union or other states, but they argued in the 22nd Session of the General Assembly that their 200 mile claims area could not be subject to the Maltese proposal because they were already under "present national jurisdiction" and therefore not even under discussion.[146]

Friedman expresses the view that the relinquishment of assets which emerging states might appropriate to a remote international agency for administration would deprive the less developed nations of their ultimate weapon—flexibility of response. Moreover, he states that the Soviet Union has clearly interposed serious objections to any and all plans that would have an international agency manage the seabed for the benefit of mankind generally.[147] So-called model proposals have failed to confront all problems of the ocean. "Some were designed to deal with only one—often one small suboptimal part—of the future status of the oceans. Others have been far too ambitious and too careless of the constraints of the real world." In all probability no single proposal will "dominate the future legal and organizational status of the oceans." Friedman is pessimistic concerning the creation of "a full-blown ocean agency which 'owns' the seabed, can lease it or regulate it at will, and, without constraint, can collect, and disburse revenues." It is possible that the actual management of marine resources will be directed by the administrative successors of the national and international functionalists, especially with respect to the dilemmas of seabed resources and fishery controls. The competence of such management is based upon experience, technical capability, and respect for state authority. The resultant may be a pragmatic division of authority between national and international agencies.[148]

When the lack of unanimity reflected in various proposals presented by jurists, academicians, and national and international authorities is considered, it seems doubtful that a viable design can soon be formulated for a regime with multinational acceptance to regulate the use of the indivisible common resource—the world ocean.

NOTES

CHAPTER ONE

1. C. A. M. King, *An Introduction to Oceanography* 311 (1966); R. C. Miller, *The Sea* 248-53 (1966); D. B. Ericson and C. Wollin, *The Ever-Changing Sea* 3-38 (1968).

2. T. F. Gaskell, *World beneath the Oceans* 21 (1964); see also H. U. Sverdrup, M. W. Johnson, and R. H. Fleming, *The Oceans: Their Physics, Chemistry and General Biology* 2 (1942); E. Guillion, "Introduction: New Horizons at Sea," in *Uses of the Seas* 2 (E. Guillion ed. 1968).

3. Gaskell, *supra* note 2, at 10; J. L. Mero, *The Mineral Resources of the Sea* 127-41 (1965); H. W. Menard, *Marine Geology of the Pacific* 170-90 (1964); N. Carlisle, *Riches of the Sea* 10, 68-70, 83 (1967).

4. Gaskell, *supra* note 2, at 23. This cruise was also significant because of the scientific contributions of Sir John Murray, a geologist, and the chief scientist, Sir Wyville Thompson. Fifty volumes were written concerning the expedition. P. Frye, A. Maxwell, K. Emery, and B. Ketchum, "Ocean Science and Marine Resources," in *Uses of the Seas* 21.

The internal structure of manganese nodules is irregularly stratified or concentric with divisions of different mineralogy ranging in color from black to brown. The center nucleus may be a piece of pumice, a small stone, or a shark tooth. Several different manganese minerals are enclosed in the nodules, all oxides of the metal. It is said that the layered arrangement is the result of changes in rate and nature of deposition during the estimated millions of years of existence of each nodule. H. B. Stewart, Jr., *The Global Sea* 15-16 (1963); R. Crum, "Harvests of the Future," in James Dugan, *World beneath the Sea* 173-77 (National Geographic Society ed. 1967).

A. Pardo, "Who Will Control the Seabed?" 47 *Foreign Affairs* 123-37 (1968). For a succinct historical account of salient historical data concerning explorations of the sea together with the development of oceanography as a *systematic* science in the first part of the nineteenth century see G. Neumann and W. Pierson, Jr., *Principles of Physical Oceanography* 2-12 (1966). The authors indicate the urgent need for depth measurement. After the invention of the electromagnetic telegraph by Gauss and Weber in 1833 and its practical application by Morse, there was the formidable task of laying electrical cables across the sea floor. Also, needs for directions and charts arose, and practical uses of the sea were accelerated by the location of favorable paths across its surface. General knowledge concerning winds, waves, cyclonic turbulences, currents, fog occurrence, the distribution of ice, and other oceanographic data was of great importance for navigational efficiency and safety measures. The fascinating account of Matthew Fontaine Maury (1806-1873), "the pathfinder of the seas," is also included. He recognized the need for international cooperation and was considered the world's foremost authority on "sea lanes." See also W. A. Hearn, "The Fourth Dimension of Sea Power: Ocean Technology and International Law," 22 *JAG J.* 23-26 (1967). Concerning authigenic minerals, the two major ones are phosphorite and manganese nodules (formed by chemical precipitation from sea water). Frye, Maxwell, Emery, and Ketchum, *supra* at 34, 36. The major use for manganese, comprising approximately 95 percent of its consumption, is as an additive metal in steel making. It serves effectively in the reduction of brittleness caused by excessive sulfur. Other substitutes are available for manganese; however, no other material accomplishes as much at minimum costs. The cost of manganese seldom exceeds 4¢ per pound, while usable substitutes such as vanadium and the rare-earth metals exceed $1.00 per pound. Economic projections indicate a continuing elevation of *total* demand for manganese due to increased world demand for steel. D. Brooks, "Deep Sea Manganese Nodules: From Scientific Phenomenon to World Resources," *Proceedings of the Second Annual Conference of the Second Annual Law of the Sea Institute* 33 (University of Rhode Island, June 26-29, 1967).

5. Evans, "Marine Geologists Drill under Atlantic for Tips," *Dallas Morning News*, Nov. 6, 1968, at 22A, col. 2; 65 *Life*, Oct. 4, 1968, at 65-76B; 33 *Look*, Jan. 21, 1969, at 68-74; S. Hull, *The Bountiful Sea* 2 (1964). Mr. Hull states that 326 million cubic miles in area comprise the waters of the earth, the ocean alone encompassing 317 million cubic miles. Wiggins, "U.S. Explains Proposal for International Decade of Ocean Exploration," 59 *Dep't State Bull.* 574, 576 (1968). Ambassador Wiggins states that theoretically precise information is ascertainable as to the location of the resources in the more than 100 million square miles of the deep ocean floor, what they contain, and the feasibility of retrieval at acceptable economic factors. Cost differentials increase materially with increasing depths of water; moreover, the task of research concerning the marine environment is monumental, of worldwide dimensions, and requires worldwide concentration of effort. Significant surveys could establish the broad dimension and character of the seabed and delineate geological provinces favorable for the occurrence of potentially valuable minerals.

6. Sverdrup, Johnson, and Fleming, *supra* note 2, at 7.

7. T. W. Fulton, *The Sovereignty of the Sea* 66 (1911).

8. J. B. Scott, Introductory Note to H. Grotius, *The Freedom of the Seas*, at viii (1916); H. Grotius, *The Freedom of the Seas* 7, 28-39 (1916); address by W. Griffin, delivered before the International Academy of Trial Lawyers, Feb. 17, 1967.

9. Fulton, *supra* note 7, at 4.

10. *Id.*

11. *Mare Liberum.* "The sea free. The title of a work written by Grotius against the Portuguese claim to an exclusive trade to the Indies, through the South Atlantic and Indian oceans, showing the sea was not capable of private domain." *Black's Law Dictionary* 1119 (4th ed. 1951).

12. *Mare Clausum.* "The sea closed; that is, not open or free. The title of Selden's great work, intended as an answer to the *Mare Liberum* of Grotius, in which he undertakes to prove the sea to be capable of private dominion." *Id.*

13. Fulton, *supra* note 7, at 106.

14. H. A. Smith, *The Law and Custom of the Sea* 58-59 (3rd ed. 1959).

15. Fulton, *supra* note 7, at 106.

16. *Id.* at 339.

17. *Id.* at 105.

18. J. L. Brierly, *The Law of Nations* 19-28 (1928).

19. Scott, *supra* note 8; Grotius, *supra* note 8. Grotius cites several Roman authors in his discussion of the freedom of water: Cicero, in *De officiis* I, 52, "Deny no one the water that flows by"; Ovid, in *Metamorphoses* VI, "Why do you deny me water? Its use is free to all. Nature has made neither sun nor air nor waves private property; they are public gifts"; Ulpian, in *Digest* VIII, 4, 13, "They (sun, air, waves) are by nature things open to the use of all, both because in the first place they were produced by nature, and have never yet come under the sovereignty of any one, as Neratius says." Grotius comments that Ovid uses "public" in its usual meaning, not of those things "which belong to any one people, but to human society as a whole . . . things which are called 'public' are, according to the laws of the law of nations, the common property of all, and the private property of none." Grotius continues: "The air belongs to this class of things for two reasons. First, it is susceptible of occupation, and second, its common use is destined for all men. For the same reasons the sea is common to all, because it is so limitless that it cannot become a possession of anyone, and because it is adapted for the use of all, whether we consider it from the point of view of navigation or of fisheries. . . . Virgil also says that the air, the sea, and the shore are open to all men." Grotius further reiterates: ". . . since the sea is just as insusceptible of physical appropriation as the air, it cannot be attached to the possessions of any nation."

20. Fulton, *supra* note 7, at 344.

21. *Id.*

22. *Id.* at 345.

23. *Id.* at 347.

24. *Id.*

25. *Id.* at 377.

26. E. Whitworth, *The Political and Commercial Works of Charles Devanant* 98 (1771); J. W. Textor, 2 *Synopsis of the Law of Nations* 126 (1916).

27. L. Oppenheim, 1 *International Law* 584 (8th ed. 1955). In 1580, Mendoza, the Spanish ambassador to England, protested to Queen Elizabeth because

of Drake's celebrated voyage to the Pacific. The Queen's reply stated that vessels of all nations were privileged to navigate the Pacific, since the use of the sea and the air is common to all nations. Queen Elizabeth further proclaimed that no title to the ocean can be possessed by any nation, since nature permits no possessory rights of the ocean.

28. Fulton, *supra* note 7, at 371.

29. *Id.* at 373.

30. *Id.*

31. *Id.* at 374.

32. *Id.* at 369.

33. *Id.* at 377.

34. A. Higgins and C. Colombos, *The International Law of the Sea* 52 (2d rev. ed. 1951).

35. *Id.* n. 5.

36. *Id.* at 52.

37. *Id.* at 50.

38. Fulton, *supra* note 7, at 537.

39. *Id.*

40. *Id.* at 549.

41. Higgins and Colombos, *supra* note 34, at 54.

42. *Id.* at 53.

43. *Id.* n. 3.

44. *Id.* at 54; see also 23 U.N. *GAOR*, Ad Hoc Committee to Study the Peaceful Uses of the Seabed and the Ocean Floor beyond the Limits of National Jurisdiction (1968); G. W. Haight, "United Nations Affairs: Ad Hoc Committee on Seabed and Ocean Floor," 3 *The Int'l Lawyer* 22-30 (1968); M. Wilkey, "The Deep Ocean: Its Potential Mineral Resources and Problems," 3 *The Int'l Lawyer* 31-48 (1968); C. Franklin, *The Law of the Sea: Some Recent Developments* 8-32 (53 U.S. Naval War College *International Law Studies 1959-1960*, 1961); M. Sorensen, "The Law of the Sea," 1958 *Int'l Conciliation* 195-201; E. Wenk, "A New National Policy for Marine Resources," 1 *Natural Resources Lawyer*, June 1968, at 3-13.

CHAPTER TWO

1. For general data concerning the League of Nations see *Basic Documents of the United Nations* 295-303 (2d rev. ed. L. Sohn ed. 1968) [hereinafter cited as Sohn]; see also, C. Eagleton, "Covenant of the League of Nations and the Charter of the United Nations: Points of Difference," in 3 *The Strategy of World Order* 10-16 (R. Falk and S. Mendlovitz eds. 1966) [hereinafter cited as Falk and Mendlovitz]; L. Goodrich, "From League of Nations to United Nations," *id.* at 17-28; C. B. Fry, *Key-Book of the League of Nations* 15-19, 22, 24 (1923); C. Colombos, *The International Law of the Sea* 21 (6th rev. ed. 1967); F. V. Garcia-Amador, *The Exploitation and Conservation of the Resources of the Sea*, 5 (2d enlarged ed. 1959); R. Berkeley, "The Work of the League of Nations," 1921-1922 *Brit. Y.B. Int'l L.* 1950-1966; Butler, "Sovereignty and the League of Nations," 1920-1921 *Brit. Y.B. Int'l L.* 44; J. L. Brierly, *The Law of Nations* 203-7 (1928); F. D. Walters, *A History of the League of Nations* 4, 7 (1952).

2. Colombos, *supra* note 1, at 21 nn. 1 and 2, 22.

3. *Id.* at 21.

4. *Id.* at 21, 22; Butler, *supra* note 1, at 35-44; see League of Nations Report to the Council of the League of Nations on the Questions Which Appear Ripe for International Regulation 53, 279, 31-32, 33-38 (Geneva, April 20, 1927). "In virtue of its right of dominion over the whole area of its territorial waters, the riparian State possesses for itself and for its nationals the sole right of ownership over the riches of the sea. This right covers the fauna in the waters, and also everything which may be found above or below, the subsoil of the territorial sea (coral reefs, oil wells, tin mines). . . . To express the universally accepted legal conception, we must include the following article in the Convention:

"Riches of the sea, the bottom and its subsoil. Article II. In virtue of its sovereign rights over the territorial sea, the riparian State shall exercise for itself and for its nationals the sole right of taking possession of the riches of the sea, the bottom and the subsoil." A. Higgins and C. Colombos, *The International Law of the Sea* 291 (2d rev. ed. 1951).

5. H. Miller, "The Hague Codification Conference," 24 *Am. J. Int'l L.* 674-93 (1930); for general comments on the work of the League see Berkeley, *supra* note 1; this conference and convention are discussed *infra* in chap. iii.

6. Miller, *supra* note 5, at 674; for the method of delimitation proposal made by the United States see S. W. Boggs, "Delimitation of the Territorial Sea," 24 *Am. J. Int'l L.* 541-55 (1930); see also J. Reeves, "The Codification of the Law of Territorial Waters," 24 *Am. J. Int'l L.* 486-99 (1930); M. O. Hudson, "The First Conference for the Codification of International Law," 24 *Am. J. Int'l L.* 447-66 (1930); in R .W. Hale, "Territorial Waters as a Test of Codification," 24 *Am. J. Int'l L.* 65; it is stated that the law of territorial waters has been, and is, and in its nature must necessarily continue to be a thing of custom, not a statute or treaty.

7. Higgins and Colombos, *supra* note 4.

8. Walters, *supra* 1, at 312-14; for general data concerning the United Nations see G. Schwarzenberger, *A Manual of International Law* 275-92 (5th ed. 1967); for Charter of the United Nations see Sohn, *supra* note 1, at 1-25; L. Meeker, "The United Nations and Law in the World Community," in *Lectures on International Law and the United Nations* 336 (Univ. of Mich. Law School 1967); Colombos, *supra* note 4, at 650-51; for discussions concerning the United Nations see J. G. Starke, *Introduction to International Law* 515-28 (6th ed. 1967); see also L. M. Goodrich and E. Hambro, *Charter of the United Nations* 6-10, 44-46(2d rev. ed. 1949).

9. E. M. Borgese, *The Ocean Regime* 2 (Center for the Study of Democratic Institutions, Oct. 1968).

10. *Id.*

11. *Id.*

12. *Id.*

13. *Id.* at 2, 3, 4.

14. *Id.* at 4, 5, 6.

15. A. Pardo, "Who Will Control the Seabed?" 47 *Foreign Affairs* 135 (1968); Borgese, *supra* note 9; see also *Hearings on H.R. Res. 179 Before the Subcomm. on the United Nations and the Issue of Deep Ocean Resources of the House Comm. on Foreign Affairs* 90th Cong., 1st Sess. 51, 84 (1967) [hereinafter cited as *1967 Hearings*].

16. Borgese, *supra* note 9, at 6; for general data concerning the General

Assembly see Starke, *supra* note 8, at 522; see also Schwarzenberger, *supra* note 8, at 290; Goodrich and Hambro, *supra* note 8, at 25-28, 44-46; concerning Resolution 295 (IV) of the General Assembly, reestablishing the Interim Committee November 21, 1949 see Sohn, *supra* note 1, at 33-66; see F. Wilcox, "Representation and Voting in the United Nations General Assembly," in Falk and Mendlovitz, *supra* note 1, at 272-75; D. Hammarskjöld, "Two Differing Concepts of United Nations Assayed," *Id.* at 817.

17. *1967 Hearings, supra* note 15, at 50, 51; see also Starke, *supra* note 8, at 522. The General Assembly's powers and functions include the direction and supervision of international economic and social cooperation and the adoption of international conventions. However, under Article 10 of the Charter it has comprehensive competence. Schwarzenberger, *supra* note 8, at 288; see also H. Kelsen, *The Law of the United Nations: A Critical Analysis of Its Fundamental Problems* 155-218 (1950).

18. Schwarzenberger, *supra* note 8, at 289; Colombos, *supra* note 1, at 22.

19. Starke, *supra* note 8, at 522; Schwarzenberger, *supra* note 8, at 289.

20. Schwarzenberger, *supra* note 8, at 289; Starke, *supra* note 8, at 522, 523.

21. 22 U.N. *GAOR,* Supp. 16, at 14-15, U.N. Doc. A/6964 (1967).

22. U.N. Resolution on the Use of Seabed and Ocean Floor, 7 *Int'l Legal Materials* 174-76 (1968). The General Assembly adopted the resolution on December 18, 1967. The vote was affirmative, 99 in favor, no negative votes, and no abstentions.

23. G.A. Res. 2340, 22 U.N. *GAOR,* Supp. 16, at 14-15, U.N. Doc. A/6964 (1967).

24. Jacques-Yves Cousteau, *World without Sun* 6-7 (1965).

25. *Id.* at 7.

26. *Id.;* 21 U.N. *GAOR,* Second Comm. 403 (1966).

27. Cousteau, *supra* note 24, at 7; G.A. Res. 2340, 22 U.N. *GAOR,* Supp. 16, at 14-15, U.N. Doc. A/6964 (1967).

28. The ad hoc committee membership was composed of representatives from Argentina, Australia, Austria, Belgium, Brazil, Bulgaria, Canada, Ceylon, Chile, Czechoslovakia, Ecuador, El Salvador, France, Iceland, India, Italy, Japan, Kenya, Liberia, Libya, Malta, Norway, Pakistan, Peru, Poland, Romania, Senegal, Somalia, Thailand, the Union of Soviet Socialist Republics, the United Arab Republic, the United Kingdom of Great Britain and Northern Ireland, the United Republic of Tanzania, the United States of America, and Yugoslavia. See also G. W. Haight, "United Nations Affairs: Ad Hoc Committee on Seabed and Ocean Floor," 3 *The Int'l Lawyer* 22 (1968).

29. *Id.* at 22-30; Starke, *supra* note 8, at 522, 542-43; see also Goodrich and Hambro, *supra* note 8, at 49-51; Schwarzenberger, *supra* note 8, at 303-6.

30. Starke, *supra* note 8, at 542, 495.

31. Borgese, *supra* note 9, at 4.

32. L. Oppenheim, 1 *International Law* 437-39 (8th ed. 1955).

33. *1967 Hearings, supra* note 15, at 231-32.

34. *Id.* at 232.

35. 21 U.N. *GAOR,* Second Comm. 403-8 (1966); see 1092 Meeting December 7, 1966, and 987th meeting.

36. *Id.* at 406. Certain nations approved Unitar's achievements including Mr. Al-Rifaie (Kuwait), Mr. Sadi (Jordan), Mr. Devendra (Nepal), Mr. Roosevelt

(United States of America), Sir Edward Warner (United Kingdom), Mr. Olumide (Nigeria), Mr. Murgesau (Romania), Mr. Abe (Japan), Mr. Al-Agroush (Saudi Arabia), Mr. Viaud (France), and many others. G.A. Res. 1827, 17 U.N. *GAOR*, Supp. 17, at 19, U.N. Doc. A/5217 (1962).

37. G.A. Res. 2172, 21 U.N. GAOR, Supp. 16, at 32, U.N. Doc. A/6316 (1966); G.A. Res. 2187 and 2188, 21 U.N. *GAOR, Id.* at 37.

38. *Id.*, Res. 2172.

39. *Id.*

40. G.A. Res. 1934, 18 U.N. *GAOR*, Supp. 14, at 27, U.N. Doc. A/6027 (1965).

41. 20 U.N. *GAOR*, Annexes, Agenda Item No. 48, at 1, U.N. Doc. A/6027 (1965).

42. 21 U.N. *GAOR*, Annexes, Agenda Item No. 47, at 7, U.N. Doc. A/6323 (1966).

43. *Id.*, Agenda Item No. 48, at 1, 5, 6, U.N. Doc. A/6500; *1967 Hearings, supra* note 15, at 232.

44. M. S. McDougal and W. T. Burke, *The Public Order of the Oceans* 15, 16 (1962).

45. E. Skolnikoff, "The National and International Organization for the Seas," in *Uses of the Seas* 101 (E. Guillion ed. 1968).

46. McDougal and Burke, *supra* note 44.

47. Skolnikoff, *supra* note 45.

48. *Id.*

49. *Id.*

50. *Id.*

51. *Id.*

52. *Id.*; Garcia-Amador, *supra note* 1, at 5-6; *The Work of the International Law Commission* 4, 5 (United Nations 1967); M. Sorensen, "The Law of the Sea," *Int'l Conciliation*, Nov. 1958, at 195.

53. Skolnikoff, *supra* note 45; *The Work of the International Law Commission, supra* note 55, at 4.

54. See 2 U.N. *GAOR*, Annexes, at 173, U.N. Doc. A/331 (1947); *The Work of the International Law Commission, supra* note 52. The committee held thirty meetings during the period between May 12 and June 17, 1947; questions relative to the scope, functions, organization, and methods were reviewed concerning an international law commission. The rationale was in effect that conclusions of international conventions would be essential prior to achieving effect upon states. The majority view supported by the committee was that members of the international law commission should be composed of individuals of recognized competence in international law rather than representatives of governments, and that the work of the committee should be accomplished in cooperation with political authorities of respective states. In regard to prospective drafts prepared by the commission, the "Committee of Seventeen" expressed the view that decisions should be determined by the General Assembly.

55. See 2 U.N. *GAOR*, Annexes, at 173, U.N. Doc. A/331 (1947).

56. *The Work of the International Law Commission, supra* note 52, at 5. The commission has been enlarged twice, from fifteen to twenty-one in 1956 (General Assembly Resolution 1103 [XI] of December 18, 1956), and to the present twenty-five in 1961, by Assembly Resolution 1647 (XVI) of November 6, 1961.

The commission has held all its sessions (usually in early May for approximately ten weeks) in Geneva except the first meeting, held in New York in 1949, the sixth session in Paris, and a portion of its seventeeth session in Monaco in 1966.

57. *The Work of the International Law Commission, supra* note 52, at 31; see "Issues before the 23rd General Assembly," *Int'l Conciliation,* Sept. 1968, at 137.

58. *The Work of the International Law Commission, supra* note 52, at 31; General Assembly Resolution 1105 (XI) of February 21, 1957.

59. *Id.;* Garcia-Amador, *supra* note 1, at 8.

60. *Id.; supra* note 1, at 4, 5.

61. *Id.;* the conference will be considered in chap. iii of this study.

62. Address by Edward Wenk, Jr., 38th Annual International Meeting, Society of Exploration Geophysicists, Oct. 2, 1968; see also E. Wenk, "Frontiers of Maritime Law," *Proceedings of the Second Annual Conference of the Second Annual Law of the Sea Institute,* at 3-6 (University of Rhode Island, June 26-29, 1967).

63. For general discussions concerning he OAS see Ann and A. J. Thomas, Jr., *The Organization of American States* (1963) for a definitive work on the history and development aspects of the Organization; see also Pan American Union, *Background Material on the Activities in the Organization of American States Relating to the Law of the Sea,* December 1957 [hereinafter cited as Pan American Union, *Background Material*]; U.N. *Charter* art. 52, para. 1; Schwarzenberger, *supra* note 8, at 338-42; Kelsen, *supra* note 17, at 319-22; Garcia-Amador, *supra* note 1, at 6, 7.

64. Garcia-Amador, *supra* note 1, at 7.

65. McDougal and Burke, *supra* note 47, at 640; Pan American Union, *Final Act of the Fourth Meeting of the Inter-American Council of Jurists,* at 36, Doc. CIJ-43 (1959).

66. For résumé of stated positions see C. M. Franklin, *The Law of the Sea: Some Recent Developments* 242-65 (53 U.S. Naval War College International Studies 1959-1960, 1961), McDougal and Burke, *supra* note 47, at 640 n. 233.

67. Pan American Union, *Background Material, supra* note 66, at 11.

68. *Id.*

69. *Id.* at 11, 12.

70. *Id.* at 31.

71. *Id.* at 33.

72. *Id.* at 35.

73. B. MacChesney, *International Law Situation and Documents* 249-54 (51 U.S. Naval War College International Studies 1956, 1957).

74. *Id.* at 255.

75. *Id.* at 258.

CHAPTER THREE

1. F. Garcia-Amador, *The Exploitation and Conservation of the Resources of the Sea* 2 (2d enlarged ed. 1959); C. Colombos, *The International Law of the Sea* 47, 48 (6th rev. ed. 1967); A. Higgins and C. Colombos, *The International Law of the Sea* 38-39 (2d rev. ed. 1951); M. McDougal and W. Burke, *The Public Order of the Oceans* 17 (1965) which states that "Participation in ocean uses may be . . . characterized by the degree to which it is, or may be made, open to all participants in the same time period. Inclusive use is that which may

be simultaneously enjoyed by more than one participant. . . . Exclusive use is that
which is enjoyed by only one participant at a time; H. Smith, *The Law and
Custom of the Sea* 6-8 (3d ed. 1959).

2. Garcia-Amador, *supra* note 1, at 16-17.

3. *Id.* at 18.

4. *Id.* at 19.

5. *Id.*

6. *Id.*

7. Colombos, *supra* note 1, at 21.

8. Garcia-Amador, *supra* note 1, at 20 and n. 4.

9. *Id.* at 5; D.H.N. Johnson, "The Conclusions of International Conferences,"
1959 *Brit. Y.B. Int'l L.* 11-16.

10. Colombos, *supra* note 1, at 22, 103; Johnson, *supra* note 9, at 11, 14.
Higgins and Colombos, *supra* note 1, at 20.

11. Johnson, *supra* note 9, at 14-15; Colombos, *supra* note 1, at 22.

12. Colombos, *supra* note 1, at 22; see also W. R. Neblett, "The 1958 Conference on the Law of the Sea: What Was Accomplished," in *The Law of the Sea*
36-44 (L. Alexander ed. 1967).

13. United Nations, *The Work of the International Law Commission* 32
(1967); Johnson, *supra* note 9, at 16-17; The British Institute of International and
Comparative Law Series No. 3, Special Publication No. 6, *Developments in the
Law of the Sea 1958-1964* 1, 13-26, 32-35 (1965) [hereinafter cited as *Develop-
ments in the Law of the Sea*]; D. W. Bowett, *The Law of the Sea* 4 (1967);
C. M. Franklin, *International Law Studies 1959-1960* 1-4 (1961).

14. *The Work of the International Law Commission, supra* note 13.

15. *Id.* at 33.

16. "Report of the International Law Commission to the General Assembly,"
2 *Y.B. Int'l L. Comm'n.* 254-301, U.N. Doc. A/3159 (1956); see *The Work of
the International Law Commission, supra* note 13, at 33.

17. *Id.* at 33.

18. *The Work of the International Law Commission, supra* note 13, at 33,
34; see Hearings on H.R. 179 before the Subcomm. on the United Nations and
the Issue of Deep Ocean Resources of the House Comm. on Foreign Affairs, 90
Cong., 1st Sess. 50-62 (1967). See also David H. Popper, Deputy Assistant
Secretary of State for International Organization Affairs, in *Interim Report on the
United Nations and the Issue of Deep Ocean Resources*, H.R. 999, 90th Cong.,
1st Sess. 50-62 (1967). Mr. Popper commented that the high seas and the
resources thereof have been regarded as international in principle, enumerating
accomplishments of the U.N. Int'l. Law Comm. and the Law of the Sea Conventions which were adopted at the 1958 Conference held in Geneva. Further, he
recalled that one of the conventions, dealing with the continental shelf, recognized the sovereign rights of coastal states for explorative purposes and for the
exploitation of natural resources of the shelf. The convention defined the shelf as
the seabed adjacent to the coast and beyond the territorial sea "to a depth of 200
meters or, beyond that limit, to where the depth of the superjacent waters admits
of the exploitation of the natural resources of the said areas." Mr. Popper re-
marked that there is presently a need for guidance in regard to the deep sea floor.
He enumerated the duplications, within the United Nations, of various bodies
engaged in the study of marine questions, namely the U.N. Educational, Scien-

tific, and Cultural Organization (UNESCO), through the Intergovernmental Oceanographic Commission (IOC) which has activated scientific programs in the area of oceanography. The World Meteorological Organization (WMO) has surveyed data pertaining to the influence of the oceans on weather conditions. The U.N. Economic and Social Council (ECOSOC) has requested the secretary-general of the United Nations to investigate the current status of knowledge concerning the resources of the sea existing beyond the continental shelf and the technological methods for the exploitation of these resources (except for fish).

In December, 1966, the United Nations General Assembly endorsed the study and requested the secretary-general to include a survey of activities in marine science and technology together with mineral resources development, initiated by the United Nations, by member states, and by private entities. A request was made for the formulation of proposals for amplification in international cooperative programs for marine science, marine education, and training. The secretary-general's report was scheduled for submission to the 23rd U.N. General Assembly.

19. Conference on the Law of the Sea, Second United Nations Conference on the Law of the Sea, U.N. Doc. A/Conf. 13/38 143-45 (1958); see U.N. Doc. A/Conf. 19/w (1960); Colombos, *supra* note 1, at 109.

20. Franklin, *supra* note 13, at 1. The paramount objective of the Geneva Conference of 1958 on the Law of the Sea, to reach concurrence on maximum utilization of oceanic areas, two-thirds of the earth's surface and the resources contained therein, represented a significant purpose. The participants in the conference included: Afghanistan, Albania, Argentina, Australia, Austria, Belgium, Bolivia, Brazil, Bulgaria, Burma, Byelorussian Soviet Socialist Republic, Cambodia, Canada, Ceylon, Chile, China (Republic of China referred to in text and footnotes as China), Colombia, Costa Rica, Cuba, Czechoslovakia, Denmark, Dominican Republic, Ecuador, El Salvador, Finland, France, Germany (Federal Republic of), Ghana, Greece, Guatemala, Haiti, Holy See, Honduras, Hungary, Iceland, India, Indonesia, Iran, Iraq, Ireland, Israel, Italy, Japan, Jordan, Korea (Republic of), Laos, Lebanon, Liberia, Libya, Luxembourg, Malaya (Federation of), Mexico, Monaco, Morocco, Nepal, Netherlands, New Zealand, Nicaragua, Norway, Pakistan, Panama, Paraguay, Peru, Philippines, Poland, Portugal, Romania, San Marino (Republic of), Saudi Arabia, Spain, Sweden, Switzerland, Thailand, Tunisia, Turkey, Ukrainian Soviet Socialist Republic, Union of South Africa, Union of Soviet Socialist Republics, United Arab Republic, United Kingdom of Great Britain and Northern Ireland, United States of America, Uruguay, Venezuela, Vietnam (Republic of), Yemen, Yugoslavia. Specialized agencies: International Labour Organization, United Nations Food and Agriculture Organization, United Nations Education, Scientific and Cultural Organization, International Civil Aviation Organization, World Health Organization, International Telecommunication Union, World Meteorological Organization.

It will be remembered that the Hague Codification Conference of 1930 concentrated on one area of the law of the sea, namely territorial water, while the Geneva Conference of 1958 encompassed major aspects of the seas together with their resources. The conference failed to reach agreement on significant issues, among them the breadth of the territorial sea, coastal fisheries, nuclear tests on the high seas, and the regimes of historic waterways. The four conventions which were adopted indicated accord among states represented by the conference. Concerning the continental shelf, seven substantive draft articles were submitted and approved by an affirmative vote of 57, 3 negative votes, and 8 abstentions. The Convention on the High Seas was adopted by 65 affirmative votes, no opposing votes, and one abstention. The result of the Conference on the Territorial Sea and Contiguous Zone was 61 in the affirmative, no opposition vote, and 2 abstentions. See also Bowett, *supra* note 13, at 4-12; Colombos, *supra* note 1, at 108-11; McDougal and Burke, *supra* note 1, at 562; Smith, *supra* note 1, at 8.

21. Franklin, *supra* note 13, at 4. The conference also constitutes the initial United Nations Codification Conference. Greater endorsement was acquired for the conventions on the high seas and the continental shelf than for the two remaining conventions; Bowett, *supra* note 13.

22. Bowett, *supra* note 13, 5 n. 1; see also 2 *International Legal Materials* 524 (1963).

23. Garcia-Amador, *supra* note 1, at 70; G. Schwarzenberger, *A Manual of International Law* 138-39, 140 (5th ed. 1967).

24. M. W. Mouton, *The Continental Shelf* (1952).

25. *Id.*

26. Starke, *Introduction to International Law* 196 (6th ed. 1967); Laughton, "The Floor of the Sea," in *Oceans* 195 (2d G. Deacon ed. 1968).

27. Mouton, *supra* note 24, at 16.

28. *Id.* at 17.

29. Franklin, *supra* note 13, at 12, 13.

30. *Id.* at 13; see H. Sverdrup, M. Johnson, and R. Fleming, *The Oceans* 9-15. (1942). Franklin calculated that the total surface of the earth is approximately 197 million square miles; of this total the oceanic area covers approximately 139 million square miles. The land mass remaining is 58 million square miles. The submarine areas beneath the oceans composed of the continental and insular shelves are about 10.5 million miles, and the continental slopes and deep ocean areas total 128.5 million square miles. Franklin, *supra* note 13, at 14.

31. Sverdrup, Johnson, and Fleming, *supra* note 30.

32. Franklin, *supra* note 13, at 15; Mouton, *supra* note 24, at 23; Bowett, *supra* note 13, at 28-29.

33. Franklin, *supra* note 13, at 17.

34. *Id.*

35. *Id.*; H. W. Menard, *Marine Geology of the Pacific* 224, 225 (1964).

36. Sverdrup, Johnson, and Fleming, *supra* note 30, at 27; Franklin, *supra* note 13, at 18.

37. Sverdrup, Johnson, and Fleming, *supra* note 30, at 21.

38. F. Jessup, *The Law of Territorial Waters and Maritime Jurisdiction* 15 (1927).

39. T. W. Fulton, *The Sovereignty of the Sea* 697, 698 (1911); Jessup, *supra* note 38, at 14, 15.

40. Jessup, *supra* note 38, at 14, 15, 16; see Anna Kumaru Pallai v. Mathupayal, XXVII Indian Law Reports, Madras Series, 551, 553 (1903).

41. Fulton, *supra* note 39, at 560, 561.

42. Franklin, *supra* note 13, at 31, 32.

43. *Id.* at 31; Smith, *supra* note 1, at 55.

44. Smith, *supra* note 1, at 82.

45. *Id.*; Franklin, *supra* note 13, at 32.

46. Franklin, *supra* note 13, at 32.

47. *Id.* at 33; see Brief for Texas, United States v. Texas, 339 U.S. 707 (1950). A drawing appears opposite page 5 of the brief delineating an area of the submarine coal mines of Lota, Chile, indicating a mine extending a four-mile distance from shore under the Pacific Ocean.

48. Starke, *supra* note 26, at 196-200; Franklin, *supra* note 13, at 34.

49. See Geneva Convention on the Continental Shelf, U.N. Doc. A/Conf. 13/L. 55, Art. 3-5 (1958).

50. Starke, *supra* note 26, at 197.

51. Smith, *supra* note 1, at 3, 4, 5; Garcia-Amador, *supra* note 1, at 13, 14; see also Jessup, *supra* note 38, at 75; see Fenn, "Origins of the Theory of Territorial Waters," 20 *Am. J. Int'l L.* 465-82 (1926).

52. Garcia-Amador, *supra* note 1, at 14; Smith, *supra* note 1, at 6, 7; Mc-Dougal and Burke, *supra* note 1, at 42.

53. Smith, *supra* note 1, at 6, 7; Colombos, *supra* note 1, at 113; see also S. W. Boggs, "Delimitation of the Territorial Sea," 25 *Am. J. Int'l L.* 541-55 (1931).

54. Schwarzenberger, *supra* note 23, at 95; Smith, *supra* note 1, at 6, 7; L. Oppenheim, 1 *International Law* 460, 461 (8th ed. 1955).

55. McDougal and Burke, *supra* note 1, at 31, 33; Smith, *supra* note 1, at 7.

56. Higgins and Colombos, *supra* note 1, at 61; Starke, *supra* note 26, at 191, 192, 208; Jessup, *supra* note 38, at xxxiv; McDougal and Burke, *supra* note 1, at 31; Schwarzenberger, *supra* note 23, at 104; A. H. Dean, "The General Conference on the Law of the Sea: What Was Accomplished," 54 *Am. J. Int'l L.* 621 (1960).

57. Schwarzenberger, *supra* note 23, at 95, 96; Oppenheim, *supra* note 54, at 452; McDougal and Burke, *supra* note 1, at 31. The most extensive claim, now generally dishonored, is the demand for unrestricted discretion to determine the breadth according to the need of the coastal state based upon a unilateral decision by such state. The majority of the claims are more reasonable in limiting the breadth to the permissible extent based upon international law. The overwhelming majority of these claims recognize a breadth limited to twelve miles; however, certain states claim a territorial sea extendible to two hundred miles. There is diversity in the claims for three- and twelve-mile breadths for the territorial sea.

58. Garcia-Amador, *supra* note 1, at 22; Schwarzenberger, *supra* note 23, at 96.

59. Higgins and Colombos, *supra* note 1, at 62; "Conference on the Law of the Sea," *supra* note 19.

60. *Id.*

61. Garcia-Amador, *supra* note 1, at 18, 22; it is admitted that the bed of the waters, as well as the subsoil beneath the territorial sea and also the internal waters, is possessed in an unlimited degree by the state which has jurisdiction or sovereignty over the surface territory. Such state, therefore, has the inherent right to exploit the surface and its subsoil by tunneling and mining for minerals. All waters beyond territorial seas are regarded as comprising a portion of the high sea.

62. McDougal and Burke, *supra* note 1, at 234; Convention on the Territorial Sea and the Contiguous Zone, U.N. Doc. A/Conf. 13/L. 52 (1958).

63. Starke, *supra* note 26, at 191.

64. *Id.* at 190

65. *Id.*

66. *Id.* at 191.

67. Franklin, *supra* note 13, at 84, 85, 86.

68. *Id.* at 85.

69. Dean, *supra* note 56 at 623, 624.

70. "The Law of the Sea," *1958 Int'l and Comparative L.Q.* Special Supplement 9, 10.

71. Franklin, *supra* note 13, at 86, 87.

72. *Id.* at 88; Address by W. Griffin before the International Academy of Trial Lawyers, Feb. 17, 1967.

73. Jessup, *supra* note 38, at 3; Griffin, *supra* note 72; see also Bernfeld, "Exploitation of Minerals in and under the Seas under Sanction of Law: The Geneva Conventions of 1958 and Beyond," in *Symposium on Private Investors Abroad* 337 (Southwestern Legal Foundation 1967); Phleger, "Recent Developments Affecting the Regime of the High Seas," 32 *Am. J. Int'l L.* 935 (1955).

74. Jessup, *supra* note 38, at 9; Starke, *supra* note 26, at 241.

75. Starke, *supra* note 26, at 22; See also Phleger, *supra* note 73 at 935; Oppenheim, *supra* note 54.

76. "The Convention on the High Seas," adopted by the United Nations Conference on the Law of the Sea, April 29, 1958, U.N. Doc. A/Conf. 13/L. 53; J. L. Mero, *The Mineral Resources of the Sea* 287 (1965); see also W. Friedman, "The Race to the Bottom of the Sea," 12 *Columbia Forum* 18 (1969); see also Phleger, *supra* note 73, at 934-35; Young, "The Legal Regime of the Deep Sea Floor," 62 *Am. J. Int'l L.* 641 (1968); see also M. Wilkey, "The Deep Ocean, Its Potential Mineral Resources and Problems," 3 *Int'l Lawyer* 31, 35 (1968). Mr. Wilkey mentions the uncertainty of the location of boundary between the continental shelf of the coastal state and the international deep ocean floor. He also mentions the variance in local boundaries and the nonacceptance by certain nations of pertinent boundaries set forth by international law, i.e., the width of the territorial sea at three to twelve miles, a contiguous zone of twelve miles, the rights of all nations to freedom of the seas beyond these limits, and the continental shelf of the 1958 Geneva Convention. (Peru, Ecuador, and Chile have asserted sovereign rights within a distance of two hundred miles into the Pacific. Argentina, by unilateral declaration, has exceeded sovereign rights over its continental shelf for limited purposes set forth in the language of the Geneva Convention, and has proclaimed sovereignty over this broad area.) Starke reiterates that navigation on the high seas was initially open to all, but during the periods of great maritime discoveries in the fifteenth and sixteenth centuries powerful maritime states (Portugal, Spain, and Great Britain) exercised sovereignty tantamount to ownership over specific areas of the open sea. These claims were adamantly protested by Hugo Grotius, who regarded the sea as *res gentium* or *res extra commercium.*

77. Phleger, *supra* note 73, at 935.

78. Schwarzenberger, *supra* note 23, at 104.

79. O. J. Lissitzyn, *International Law Today and Tomorrow* 17-20 (1965); see also Sorensen, "National Sovereignty over the Marginal Sea" in 520 *International Conciliation* 233, 234 (1958); concerning innocent passage see Dean, *supra* note 56, at 621-23.

80. Garcia-Amador, *supra* note 1, at 52.

81. McDougal and Burke, *supra* note 1, at 179.

82. Lissitzyn, *supra* note 79; see also Sorensen, *supra* note 79.

83. McDougal and Burke, *supra* note 1, at 179.

84. J. Reeves, "The Codification of the Law of Territorial Waters," 24 *Am. J. Int'l L.* 486 (1930).

85. *Id.*

86. *Id.* at 498-99.

87. Garcia-Amador, *supra* note 1, at 5.

88. *Id.* at 6.

89. *Id.* at 8.

90. *Id.*

91. *Id.*

92. *Id.* at 22, 23; see also D. O'Connell, 1 *International Law* 523-26 (1965).

93. Garcia-Amador, *supra* note 1, at 22.

94. *Id.*

95. *Id.*

96. *Id.* at 24.

97. *Id.* at 25.

98. *Id.*

99. *Id.* at 26.

100. Jessup, *supra* note 38, at 3, 4; Oppenheim, *supra* note 54, at 584; Starke, *supra* note 26, at 241.

101. Oppenheim, *supra* note 54, at 583; Starke, *supra* note 26, at 241.

102. A. L. Shalowitz, *Shore and Sea Boundaries* 24, 25 (1962).

103. *Id.* at 25; Heingen, "The Three-Mile Limit: Preserving the Freedom of the Seas," 11 *Stanford Law Review* 597-664 (1959); see also Cunard S.S. Co. v. Mellon, 262 U.S. 100, 124, 27 *A.L.R.* 1306, 1316 (1923); see also The Schooner Exchange v. McFadden, 11 U.S. (7 Cranch) 116, 137 (1812 dictum). The following studies provide an informative background on the origins of the three-mile limit: Grogan v. Walker, 259 U.S. 80 (1921); S. Oda, *International Control of Sea Resources* 13 (1963); T. Baty, "The Three Mile Limit," 22 *Am. J. Int'l L.* 503 (1928); H. Kent, "The Historical Origins of the Three-Mile Limit," 48 *Am. J. Int'l L.* 537-53 (1954).

104. Kent, *supra* note 103, at 552-53.

105. *Id.*

106. Baty, *supra* note 103, at 515-16; Heingen, *supra* note 103; see also Jessup, *supra* note 38, at 39; Oda, *supra* note 103.

107. Heingen, *supra* note 103, at 600.

108. *Id.*

109. *Id.* at 602.

110. *Id.*

111. *Id.* n. 16, citing J. B. Scott, "Introduction to Bynkershoek," *De Domino Maris Dissertatio* 17 (Scott ed. 1923).

112. Heingen, *supra* note 103, at 605.

113. *Id.* at 613, 618; see The Schooner Exchange v. McFadden, *supra* note 103.

114. Heingen, *supra* note 103, at 619.

115. *Id.* at 614.

116. *Id.* at 629. Spain was the only country which entered a claim for more than the three-mile zone of general jurisdiction on territorial sea during the greater part of the nineteenth century; Lissitzyn, *supra* note 103, at 613.

117. Jessup, *supra* note 38, at 75.

118. E. D. Dickenson, "Jurisdiction at the Maritime Frontier," 40 *Harv. L. Rev.* 1, 14-16 (1926).

119. Church v. Hubbart, 6 U.S. (2 Cranch) 187, 234, 235 (1804).

120. Sorensen, *supra* note 79, at 252.

121. Heingen, *supra* note 103, at 639.

122. Sorensen, *supra* note 79, at 242.

123. *Id.*

124. *Id.* at 242.

125. Heingen, *supra* note 103, at 623.

126. *Id.* at 642.

127. *Id.* at 597.

128. *Id.* at 598.

129. *Id.* at 643, n. 216.

130. *Id.* at 646, n. 217; Phleger, *supra* note 73, at 935.

131. Phleger, *supra* note 130; Colombos, *supra* note 1, at 98, 99.

132. Franklin, *supra* note 13, at 50-63; Heingen, *supra* note 103, at 216, 217; R. Young, "Recent Developments with Respect to the Continental Shelf," 42 *Am. J. Int'l L.* 849, 853-54 (1948).

133. Phleger, *supra* note 73, at 935; see also Garcia-Amador, *supra* note 1, at 98-100.

134. O'Connell, *supra* note 92, at 319; see also E. Vattel, *The Law of Nations* xiii (Chitty ed. 1835) in which he states that the law of nations is the law of sovereigns and is a science which teaches the rights existing between nations or states and the obligations corresponding to these rights.

135. O'Connell, *supra* note 92, at 319; see (concerning state territory) Oppenheim, *supra* note 54, at 451, 452.

136. O'Connell, *supra* note 92, at 533.

137. *Id.* at 533, 534.

138. *Id.* at 534.

139. *Id.*

140. This position conforms to views expressed by Bynkershoek; see O'Connell, *supra* note 92, at 535, n. 40; Smith, *supra* note 1, at 45.

141. H. Lauterpacht, "Sovereignty over Submarine Areas," in 27 *Brit. Y.B. Int'l L.* 376, 387 (1950); see Jessup, *supra* note 38, at 116; Smith, *supra* note 1, at 45.

142. O'Connell, *supra* note 92, at 535; Convention on the Territorial Seas, *supra* note 62; Schwarzenberger, *supra* note 23, at 64-65.

143. W. T. Burke, *International Legal Problems of Scientific Research in the Oceans* (1967).

144. *Id.*; W. A. Hearn, "The Fourth Dimension of Seapower: Ocean Technology and International Law," 22 *Navy JAG Journal*, Special Issue, 23 (1967).

145. H. Gimlin, "Sea as Source of Food for Multiplying Millions in Oceans and Man," 1 *Editorial Research Reports* 329-30 (1968).

146. Burke, *supra* note 144, at 10-11.

147. *Id.* at 11, n. 28.

148. J. Stratton, "Foreword," in *Uses of the Sea* xiv (1968).

149. *Id.*; E. Wenk, "A New National Policy for Marine Resources," in 1 *Natural Resources Lawyer* 3, 5 (1968).

150. Stratton, *supra* note 148, at xv.

151. L. A. Alexander, "Offshore Claims of the World," in *The Law of the Sea* 84 (Alexander ed. 1967).

152. J. Robertson, "Security, Interests, and Regimes of the Sea" in *The Law of the Sea: Proceedings of the Second Annual Conference of the Second Annual Law of the Sea Institute* 47 (1967).

153. Comm. on Oceanography, Nat'l Research Council, Nat'l Academy of Sciences and the Comm. on Ocean Engineering, Nat'l Academy of Engineering, *An Oceanic Quest* 6 (1969).

154. Marine Resources and Engineering Development Act of 1966, 80 Stat. 203 (1966).

155. *Id.*

156. S. Udall, *A Plan for the Accelerated Development of Marine Natural Resources* 1-19, a presentation to the Nat'l Council on Marine Resources and Engineering Development, Jan. 18, 1967; the national policy was set forth in the Marine Resources and Development Act of 1966 (80 Stat. 203). The act stated in section 2 (a) that the policy of the United States would be to develop, encourage, and maintain a coordinated, comprehensive, long-range program in marine science for the benefit of mankind, to assist in the protection of health and property, and the enhancement of commerce, transportation, and national security, and to increase utilization of these and other resources. The purpose of the act was to accelerate development of resources of the marine environment and to encourage private investment enterprise in exploration, marine commerce, and economic utilization of marine resources.

157. C. H. Burgess, "Needs of the Mineral Industry" in *The Law of the Sea: Proceedings of the Third Annual Conference of the Third Annual Law of the Sea Institute* 327, 329 (1968); F. Christy, "Minerals of the Deep Sea," in *Id.* at 331-33; Mero, *supra* note 76, at 275.

158. *Id.* at 275, 276, 277, 279, 280.

159. *Id.* at 277; K. D. Emery, "The Continental Shelf and Its Mineral Resources," in *Selected Papers from the Governor's Conference on Oceanology*, 36, 46 (1967).

160. Pardo, "Who Will Control the Sea-bed?" 47 *Foreign Affairs* 124 (1968).

161. Bernfield, *supra* note 73, at 337, 368.

162. Report of the Comm. on Marine Science, Engineering, and Resources, *Our Nation and the Sea*, H.R. Doc. No. 91-42, 91st Congress, 1st Session 158 (1969).

163. *Id.*

164. *Id.* at 161; see also K. Emery, P. Frye, B. Ketchum, and A. Maxwell, "Ocean Science and Marine Resources," in *Uses of the Sea* 30 (1968).

165. Young, *supra* note 76, at 642.

166. *Id.*

167. Emery et al., *supra* note 164, at 31.

168. *Id.* at 32.

169. *Id.* at 33; see also Comm. on Oceanography, Div. of Earth Sciences, Nat'l Academy of Sciences, Nat'l Research Council, *Oceanography 1966* 44 (1967);

concerning deep sea sediments, see T. F. Gaskell, *Under the Deep Oceans* 53, 112, 152, 153.

170. "Ocean Science and Marine Resources," *supra* note 164, at 33.

171. L. Henkin, "Changing Law for the Changing Seas," in *Uses of the Sea*, 87 (1968).

172. N. McLean, "The Economics of Marine Science," in *Selected Papers from the Governor's Conference on Oceanography* 156 (1967).

173. *Id.* at 158.

174. *Id.* at 158-59.

175. *Id.* at 159.

176. *Id.*; see also McDonald, "An American Strategy for the Oceans," in *Uses of the Sea* 167 (1968).

177. McLean, *supra* note 172, at 159; see also "Ocean Science and Marine Resources," *supra* note 164, at 68.

178. C. Hurst, "Whose Is the Bed of the Sea" 4 *Brit. Y.B. Int'l L.* 34 (reprinted 1962); on page 37, Hurst states, "The rights of the Crown in the bed of the sea must have been fixed at least as early as the thirteenth century." Franklin, *supra* note 13, at 30; Jessup, *supra* note 38.

179. Hurst, *supra* note 178.

180. *Id.* at 34, n. 1.

181. Hurst, *supra* note 178.

182. *Id.* at 35-36.

183. *Id.* at 36.

184. *Id.* at 37.

185. Franklin, *supra* note 13, at 33, 34.

186. *Id.*

187. *Id.* at 34.

188. *Id.* at 37; McDougal and Burke, *supra* note 1, at 535-36; see also G. Hackworth, 11 *Digest of International Law* 679-80 (1941).

189. Franklin, *supra* note 13, at 37.

190. Presidential Proclamation 2667, September 28, 1945, with Respect to Natural Resources of the Subsoil and Seabed of the Continental Shelf, 10 Fed. Reg. 12303 (1945); see also E. Bocchard, "Resources of the Continental Shelf," 40 *Am. J. Int'l L.* 53 (1946); E. Lauterpacht, "Sovereignty over Submarine Areas," 27 *Brit. Y.B. Int'l L.* 376, 377 (1950); H. Holland, "Judicial Status of the Continental Shelf," 30 *Texas L. Rev.* 586 (1952); S. Oda, "A Reconsideration of the Continental Shelf Doctrine," 32 *Tul. L. Rev.* 21 (1957); Mouton, *supra* note 24; C. Selak, "Recent Developments in High Seas Fishery Jurisdiction under the Presidential Proclamation of 1945," 44 *Am. J. Int'l L.* 670 (1950); F. Yallat, "The Continental Shelf," in 23 *Brit. Y.B. Int'l L.* 333 (1946); R. Young, "Recent Developments with Reference to the Continental Shelf," 42 *Am. J. Int'l L.* 849 (1948); Udall, *supra* note 156, at 12.

191. W. W. Bishop, *International Law* 535-36 (2d ed. 1962); Presidential Proclamation, *supra* note 190.

192. McDougal and Burke, *supra* note 1, at 636; Franklin, *supra* note 13, at 38-40.

193. Fenwick, *supra* note 100, at 423; Colombos, *supra* note 1, at 71.

194. Starke, *supra* note 26, at 197.

195. *Id.* at 198.

196. See Lauterpacht, *supra* note 190, at 385.

197. "Arbitration between Petroleum Development, Ltd. and Sheikh of Abu Shabi," 47 *Am. J. Int'l L.* 156-59 (1951).

198. Schwarzenberger, *supra* note 23, at 138-39.

199. Tabb, Legal Problems Involved in Offshore Drilling and Productive Operations of Mobil Oil Corporation, Dallas, Texas 4 (undated).

200. *Id.* at 4, 5, 6.

201. Colombos, *supra* note 1, at 79.

202. F. T. Christy, "Minerals of the Deep Sea," in *The Law of the Sea: Proceedings of the Third Annual Conference of the Third Annual Law of the Sea Institute* 331 (1968).

203. Mero, *supra* note 76, at 274.

204. *Id.* at 275.

205. C. H. Burgess, "Needs of the Mineral Industry" in *The Law of the Sea, Proceedings of the Third Annual Conference of the Third Annual Law of the Sea Institute* 327-30 (1968).

206. *An Oceanic Quest, supra* note 153, at 30.

207. W. R. Hibbard, Jr., "Offshore Petroleum and Natural Gas: A Marine Resource of Increasing Importance" in *The Law of the Sea: The Future of the Sea's Resources, Proceedings of the Second Annual Conference of the Second Annual Law of the Sea Institute* 52 (1967).

208. *Id.*

209. Department of State Foreign Policy Briefs, Office of Media Services, Bureau of Public Affairs, vol. 18, no. 22, April 21, 1969. The Glomar *Challenger* made a 40,000 mile voyage; it was the first of a new category of dynamically positioned, satellite-navigated drilling ships with capacity for deep water operations. The objective of the voyage was to drill between 40 and 60 test holes in water depths ranging from 5,000 to 22,000 feet for the 18-month expedition for the National Science Foundation. The drilling derrick was 194 feet above the water line.

210. See generally B. Cooper and T. F. Gaskell, *North Sea Oil: The Great Gamble* 62, 66, 75-77 (1966); Mero, *supra* note 76, at 23.

211. *An Oceanic Quest, supra* note 153, at 10; for practical aspects of offshore mining and diversity of national policies and laws see W. Bascom, "Mining in the Sea" in *The Law of the Sea* 160-71 (Alexander ed. 1967).

212. Walthier, "Remarks on the Mining of Deep Ocean Mineral Deposits" in *The Law of the Sea: Proceedings of the Second Annual Conference of the Second Annual Law of the Sea Institute* 99 (1967).

CHAPTER FOUR

1. H. A. Smith, *The Law and Custom of the Sea* 50 (1959); A. Higgins and C. Colombos, *The International Law of the Sea* 62 (2d rev. ed. 1951); Garcia-Amador, *The Exploitation and Conservation of the Resources of the Sea* 22 (2d enlarged ed. 1959); D. W. Bowett, *The Law of the Sea* 5, 6, 13 (1967).

2. Presidential Proclamation No. 2667, Sept. 28, 1945, 59 Stat. 10 *Federal Register* 12303; M. W. Mouton, *The Continental Shelf* 32, 33 (1952).

3. *Id.*

4. *Id.* at 35.

5. *Id.* at 40, 41.

6. M. S. McDougal and W. T. Burke, "Crisis in the Law of the Sea: Community Perspective versus National Egoism," 67 *Yale L. Rev.* 539, 540 (1958); T. W. Fulton, *Sovereignty of the Sea* 544-45 (1911).

7. *Id.* at 545.

8. McDougal and Burke, *supra* note 6, at 541.

9. Mouton, *supra* note 2, at 4.

10. McDougal and Burke, *supra* note 6, at 541 n. 11; the International Law Commission adopted the criterion of exploitability for the determination of areas within the exclusive competence of the coastal state; however, adherence to some degree of propinquity was probably also intended. International Law Commission Report, U.N. General Assembly Off. Rec., 11th Sess., Supp. No. 9, art. 67. (Doc. No. A/3159) (1956).

11. McDougal and Burke, *supra* note 6, at 542-43.

12. *Id.* at 545.

13. *Id.*

14. *Id.*

15. Garcia-Amador, *supra* note 1, at 22, 23.

16. McDougal and Burke, *supra* note 6, at 546-47.

17. Garcia-Amador, *supra* note 1, at 24.

18. *Id.*

19. McDougal and Burke, *supra* note 6, at 547.

20. J. G. Starke, *Introduction to International Law* 199 (6th ed. 1967).

21. See J. A. C. Gutteridge, "The 1958 Convention on the Continental Shelf," 35 *Brit. Y.B. Int'l L.*, 103, 104, 105 (1959).

22. McDougal and Burke, *supra* note 21, at 693.

23. Gutteridge, *supra* note 21, at 693.

24. McDougal and Burke, *supra* note 6, at 694-95; Lauterpacht, "Sovereignty over Submarine Areas," 27 *Brit. Y.B. Int'l L.* 391; Young, "The Legal Status of Submarine Areas beneath the High Seas," 45 *Am. J. Int'l L.* 225, 238-39 (1951).

25. Gutteridge, *supra* note 23, at 110, n. 1.

26. *Id.* at 111.

27. Department of International Law, Pan American Union, *Background Materials on the Activities in the Organization of American States Relating to the Law of the Sea* 39-46 (1957).

28. Gutteridge, *supra* note 21, at 111.

29. E. D. Brown, "Deep-Sea Mining: The Legal Regime of 'Inner Space,'" *The Year Book of World Affairs* 185 (1968).

30. Bowett, *supra* note 1, at 37.

31. Convention on the Continental Shelf, signed at Geneva, April 29, 1958; came into force June 10, 1964; adopted by the United Nations Conference on the Law of the Sea (U.N. Doc. A/Conf. 13/L. 55).

32. Convention on the High Seas, article 2; adopted by the United Nations Conference on the Law of the Sea, April 29, 1958 (U.N. Doc. A/Conf. 13/L. 53); effective September 30, 1962.

33. Garcia-Amador, *supra* note 1, at 212, 95.

34. McDougal and Burke, *supra* note 6, at 569.

35. *Id.* at 589.

36. McDougal and Burke, *The Public Order of the Ocean* 81 (1962).

37. C. Colombos, *International Law of the Sea* 424 (6th ed. 1967).

38. *Id.* at 424, 425. See Garcia-Amador, *supra* note 1, at 126, concerning the meaning of natural resources.

39. Colombos, *supra* note 37, at 425.

40. *Id.* at 426.

41. Official Records of the General Assembly, 8th Sess. Supp. No. 9 (A/2456), 17; Colombos, *supra* note 37, at 426.

42. Garcia-Amador, *supra* note 1, at 8, 9.

43. *Id.* at 10, 11, 12.

44. J. L. Mero, *The Mineral Resources of the Sea* 290, 291 (1965).

45. W. Burke, *Ocean Sciences, Technology, and the Future International Law of the Sea* 64 (1966).

46. *Id.*

47. *Id.*

48. McDougal and Burke, *supra* note 1, at 16; The United Nations and the Bed of the Sea, Nineteenth Report of the Commission to Study the Organization of Peace (March 1969) 12; Burke, *supra* note 45, at 64.

49. E. Skolnikoff, "National and International Organization for the Seas," *Uses of the Sea* 101 (E. Guillion ed. 1968).

50. Burke, *supra* note 45, at 65.

51. Skolnikoff, *supra* note 49, at 102.

52. *Id.*

53. L. Henkin, "Changing Law for the Changing Sea" in *Uses of the Sea* 96 (E. Guillion ed. 1968).

54. Skolnikoff, *supra* note 49, at 102.

55. *Id.*

56. Henkin, *supra* note 53, at 52, 53.

57. *Id.* at 64 n. 200 and text. See also McDougal and Burke, *supra* note 6, at 681; Garcia-Amador, *supra* note 1, at 101-8 for a succinct discussion of the position of the Inter-American Organizations and Conferences. The Inter-American Organization of American States presented to the International Law Commission a definition of the continental shelf which was adopted in 1956 by the commission and was embodied in the convention.

58. Henkin, *supra* note 53, at 65.

59. W. Langeraar, "Some Thoughts on an International Regime and Administering Agency for the Seabed and the Ocean Floor beyond the Limits of National Jurisdiction" at 1. An address presented for discussion at the Fourth Law of the Sea Institute at Rhode Island University, Kingston, R.I., June 23-26, 1969.

60. F. T. Christy, Jr., "Alternate Regimes for Marine Resources Underlying the High Seas," 1 *Natural Resources Lawyer* 66 (June 1968).

61. Henkin, *supra* note 53, at 66, 67.

62. *Id.*

63. *Id.* at 68.

64. *Id.*

65. *Id.* at 67-68.

66. *Id.*

67. Christy, *supra* note 60, at 66.

68. *Id.*

69. *Id.* at 69, 70.

70. *Id.* at 74.

71. Brown, *supra* note 29, at 177.
72. *Id.* at 177-78.
73. *Id.* at 178.
74. *Id.*
75. *Id.*
76. *Id.* at 178-79.
77. *Id.* at 179.
78. Gen. Ass. Res. 2340 (XXII) and 2467 (XXIII); Comm. on Marine Science, Engineering, and Resources, *Our Nation and the Sea* (1968); A. L. Danzig and others, *Treaty Governing the Exploration and Use of the Ocean Floor* 27 pp. (undated); W. Burke, "Law, Science, and the Ocean" in Occasional Paper No. 3, August 1969 (Kingston, R.I., The Fourth Law of the Sea Institute, University of Rhode Island, February, 1969); A. Pardo, "Who Will Control the Seabed?" 47 *Foreign Affairs* 123-37 (1968); R. L. Friedman, "Understanding the Debate on Ocean Resources," Occasional Paper No. 1 (Kingston, R.I., The Fourth Law of the Sea Institute, University of Rhode Island, February, 1969).
79. Brown, *supra* note 29, at 165-90.
80. Skolnikoff, *supra* note 49, at 103.
81. Statement of Arvid Pardo, Representative of Malta, U.N. Gen. Ass., 22nd Sess., U.N. Doc. No. A/6695; U.N. Doc. No. A/AC 135/1 at 27; Provisional A/c. 1/PV. 1515 and Provisional A/c. 1 PV. 1516 of Nov. 1, 1967, English; provisional verbatim records of the 1515th and 1516th meetings.
82. H. Gimlin, "Malta's Plan for U.N. Control of Deep Seabed," 1 *Oceans and Man* 338 (1968).
83. See the Maltese agenda proposal contained in its *note verbale*, U.N. Doc. A/6695, August 18, 1967.
84. E. M. Borgese, *The Ocean Regime*. A Center Occasional Paper, The Center for the Study of Democratic Institutions, Vol. 1, No. 5, p. 3 (October 1968). S. Res. 172, 90th Cong., 1st Sess. (September 29, 1967). See also 113 Cong. Rec. S. 13875-13877 (Sept. 29, 1967); on March 5, 1968, Sen. Pell introduced a new Senate Resolution 263 containing a prospective draft treaty.
85. *Id.*
86. *Id.*
87. *Id.* at 4.
88. G. Weissberg, "International Law Meets the Short-Term National Interest: The Maltese Proposal on the Seabed and Ocean Floor—Its Fate in Two Cities," 18 *Int'l and Comparative L. Q.* 91 (January 1969).
89. Danzig Treaty, *supra* note 78.
90. 2 U.N. (7 *GAOR* 14 Vol. VI (1947)).
91. Danzig Treaty, *supra* note 78, at 9.
92. *Id.* at 13. See also McDougal and Burke, *supra* note 36, at 1108-40.
93. *Id.* at 18.
94. *Id.* at 22.
95. *Id.* at 23.
96. Borgese, *supra* note 83, at 4, 5.
97. *Id.* at 6.
98. *Id.*
99. *Id.* at 6, 8; and also the Draft Statute at 9-39 in L. F. E. Goldie, R. Johnson, A. A. Melamed, A. Alexander, J. L. Mero, H. Reiff, "A Symposium on

the Geneva Conventions and the Need for Future Modifications," *Law of the Sea*
275-92 (L. Alexander ed. 1967).

100. Henkin, *supra* note 53, at 49.

101. Christy, *supra* note 60, at 75.

102. *Id.*

103. *Id.* at 76, 77.

104. Brown, *supra* note 29, at 187, 188.

105. *Id.* at 186.

106. Henkin, *supra* note 53, at 93.

107. Brown, *supra* note 29, at 189, 190.

108. N. Ely, "A Case for the Administration of Mineral Resources Underlying the High Seas by National Interests," 1 *Natural Resources Lawyer* 81 (June
1968).

109. A. H. Dean, "The Law of the Sea Conference, 1958-1960, and Its
Aftermath" in *The Law of the Sea* 249, 250 (L. Alexander ed. 1967).

110. *Id.*

111. *Id.*

112. Goldie, *supra* note 99, at 276.

113. *Id.* at 277.

114. Dean, *supra* note 109, at 246-48; Goldie, *supra* note 99, at 277.

115. Shalowitz, *supra* note 49, at 246. This limit is approximate; the actual
shelf rim may lie above or below it.

116. Dean, *supra* note 109, at 248, 249.

117. R. Young, "Offshore Claims and Problems in the North Sea," in 59
Am. J. Int'l L. 507 (1965); see generally, Lauterpacht, *supra* note 24, at 376-433.

118. Young, *supra* note 117, at 507, 508; for a comment on multiple marine
resource development in the Gulf of Mexico see W. R. Hibbard, Jr., "Offshore
Petroleum and Natural Gas: A Marine Resource of Increasing Importance," *Law
of the Sea* 54. *Proceedings of the Second Annual Conference of the Second Annual Law of the Sea Institute* (L. Alexander ed. 1969).

119. *Id.* at 509, 511; 73-83, 89; for sea lanes, see W. L. Griffin, "Accommodation of Conflicting Uses of Ocean Space with Special Reference to Navigation Safety Lanes," in *Law of the Sea: The Future of the Sea's Resources* 79,
*Proceedings of the Second Annual Conference of the Second Annual Law of the
Sea Institute* (L. Alexander ed. 1968).

120. *Id.* at 516; see Griffin, *supra* note 119, at 76, for a discussion of factors
to be considered for the determination of unjustifiable interference.

121. *Id.*; for equitable apportionment of benefits, see Griffin, *supra* note 119,
at 77.

122. *Id.* at 518.

123. *Id.* at 520; see generally Griffin, *supra* note 119, at 73-83.

124. McDougal and Burke, *supra* note 36, at 721.

125. Young, *supra* note 117, at 522.

126. *Id.*; Goldie, *supra* note 99, at 280-81.

127. Goldie, *supra* note 99, at 281, 282, 283, 285.

128. L. Henkin, *Law for the Sea's Mineral Resources* 60 (1968).

129. *Id.* at 60, 61.

130. Ely, *supra* note 108, at 82.

131. *Id.* at 83.

132. *Id.*

133. *Id.* at 84.

134. Committee on Deep Sea Mineral Resources of the American Branch of the International Law Association, Interim Report, July 19, 1968.

135. *Id.*

136. *Id.* at xvi.

137. *Id.* at xix.

138. V. Basiuk, *Marine Resources Development, Foreign Policy, and the Spectrum of Choice* 52, 53 (1968).

139. U. A. Johnson, "Department Reviews History of International Efforts Governing Activities on the Seabed," 61 *Dept. of State Bull.* 192 (September 1, 1969).

140. W. T. Burke, "A Negative View of a Proposal for United Nations Ownership of Ocean Mineral Resources," 1 *Natural Resources Lawyer* 42, 45-46 (1968); see also entire report: The United Nations and the Bed of the Sea. Nineteenth Report of the Commission to Study the Organization of Peace 9-29 (March 1969).

141. M. S. McDougal, "International Law and the Law of the Sea," in *Law of the Sea* 3 (Alexander ed. 1967).

142. R. Young, "The Legal Regime of the Deep-Sea Floor," 62 *Am. J. Int'l L.* 651 (July 1968).

143. *Id.*; U.N. Gen. Assembly Res. 2172 (XXI), Dec. 8, 1966; see also comments concerning the Ad Hoc Committee by Rear Admiral W. Langeraar, *supra* note 59, at 23-26.

144. W. M. Chapman, *The Ocean Regime and the Real World,* presented at the Law of the Sea Institute, Univ. of Rhode Island, Kingston, R.I., June 26, 1969.

145. *Id.* at 20, 23.

146. Friedman, *supra* note 78, at 59-60. For two examples of the many attitudes of some of the Latin American states, see U.N. Doc. A/c. 1/Pv. 1526, 23-25; U.N. Doc. A/c. 1/Pv. 1527, 8-32.

147. U.N. Doc. A/c. 1/Pv. 1592, 17; Friedman, *supra* note 78, at 59, 60, 62, 63, 64.

148. Friedman, *supra* note 78, at 64.

INDEX